VOICES IN THE GALLERY

VOICES
IN THE GALLERY

Poems & Pictures chosen by

Dannie & Joan Abse

THE TATE GALLERY

ISBN 0 946590 53 2 (paper)
ISBN 0 946590 54 0 (cloth)
Copyright © 1986 The Tate Gallery All rights reserved
Designed by Caroline Johnston
Published by Tate Gallery Publications,
Millbank, London SW1P 4RG
Printed by Jolly & Barber Ltd, Rugby, Warwickshire

FRONT COVER JACKET
photograph: John Webb FRPS

Contents

Introduction

Since antiquity poetry and painting have been regarded as sister arts. Did not the poet Simonides characterise painting as mute poetry, poetry as a speaking picture? Century after century, painters and sculptors have been inspired by biblical themes; by mythological stories related by Homer, Ovid, Virgil; by the fictions of Shakespeare and other poets. How many Bathshebas have posed in artists' studios? How many Ledas about to be disgraced? How many painters have drowned Ophelia?

The converse influence of painter on poet has occurred less commonly. Or so it appeared until the 20th century when literary painting became an anathema and, because of the greater visibility of paintings in public galleries, poets turned more often than formerly to art for subject matter. Painters, of course, still occasionally acknowledge their debt to poets: Sickert to W.H. Davies; Motherwell to Lorca; Francis Bacon to T.S. Eliot; David Hockney to Wallace Stevens; Ceri Richards to Dylan Thomas – but frequently, when they do so, it is difficult to discern the relationship between their paintings and the poems they declare to be their inspirational source. We might miss the connection altogether were it not for the painting's title or the scholarly footnote in a catalogue. It could hardly be otherwise with abstract painters who have obeyed the injunction of the Austrian poet, Ernst Jandl: 'Let no field recall bread, no forest a house or wardrobe, no stone a wall . . . no pond no lake no sea a swimmer, boat, oar, sail . . . let nothing recall anything but white recall white, black black, red red, straight recall straight, round recall round.'

While the 20th-century painters' metaphors for poems may seem some-what private (we have included here but one example – Ceri Richards's response to Dylan Thomas – and this may be compared with a more overt figurative painter's response: Sickert to W.H. Davies) the 'love-affairs' of modern poets with paintings and sculpture are often unashamedly public, the relationship evident, happily undisguised.

Indeed, in compiling this anthology, we were surprised by the sheer number of such poems. Alas, most are descriptions. Only a minority of poets truly inhabit the painting that has arrested them and to which, indirectly, they pay homage. It is these poems we offer, poems that can survive the distance from their source; and yet we trust that the very adjacency of poem and picture will allow an illuminating synergy and a serious entertainment for the reader – if not always by setting his imagination free, then at least by temporarily and profitably confining it.

We have also included, perhaps impertinently, one section called 'Correspondences' where artist and poet independently dwell on a similar theme. 'As is painting so is poetry,' wrote Horace. And sometimes this is true in a way that he did not intend. In any case, we hope all the correspondences here will allow the reader double enlightenment, double pleasure.

D.A.

J.A.

AUTHORS' ACKNOWLEDGEMENTS

We should like to thank Mr Iain Bain of the Tate Gallery Publications Department whose enthusiasm for this anthology we found so encouraging and Mrs P.A. Adams of the Tate Gallery Education Department for tactfully directing us to a number of poems commissioned by the Tate Gallery: 'Sir Brooke Boothby' by Gerda Mayer; 'God Creating Adam' by D.J. Enright; 'Oi yoi yoi' by Vicki Feaver; 'A Painter Painted' by Michael Hamburger; 'The Rothko Room' by Gillian Clarke; 'J.W.M. Turner, The Shipwreck' by John Wain and 'Leaving the Tate' by Fleur Adcock. Naturally we wish to thank the poets for allowing us to reprint these poems here. We are grateful, too, to Mr James Hamilton for drawing our attention to the 1953 annual P.E.N. anthology which included Jon Manchip White's 'The Rout of San Romano'. Finally, we are indebted to Mollie Luther for her patient assistance.

PART I

THE MODERN POET AND
THE OLD MASTERS

ZBIGNIEW HERBERT

Old Masters

The Old Masters
dispensed with names

their signatures
were the white fingers of the Madonna

or pink towers
di citta sul mare

and also scenes from the life
della Beata Umiltà

they dissolved
in sogno
miracolo
crocifissione

they found refuge
under an angel's eyelid
behind hillocks of clouds
in the thick grasses of paradise

they drowned totally
in golden sunsets
without cries of terror
or pleas for remembrance

the surfaces of their paintings
are smooth like mirrors

mirrors not for us
mirrors for the elect

I call upon you Old Masters
in moments of deep despair

cause me to shed
the snake skin of pride

may I remain deaf
to temptations of fame

I call upon you Old Masters

Painter of Manna Rain
Painter of Embroidered Towers
Painter of the Visitation
Painter of the Sacred Blood
Translated by Adam Czerniawski

W.H. AUDEN

Musée des Beaux Arts

About suffering they were never wrong,
The Old Masters: how well they understood
Its human position; how it takes place
While someone else is eating or opening a window or just
    walking dully along;
How, when the aged are reverently, passionately waiting
For the miraculous birth, there always must be
Children who did not specially want it to happen, skating
On a pond at the edge of the wood:
They never forgot
That even the dreadful martyrdom must run its course
Anyhow in a corner, some untidy spot
Where the dogs go on with their doggy life and the torturer's
    horse
Scratches its innocent behind on a tree.

In Brueghel's *Icarus*, for instance: how everything turns away
Quite leisurely from the disaster; the ploughman may
Have heard the splash, the forsaken cry,
But for him it was not an important failure; the sun shone
As it had to on the white legs disappearing into the green
Water; and the expensive delicate ship that must have seen
Something amazing, a boy falling out of the sky,
Had somewhere to get to and sailed calmly on.

Pieter Brueghel the Elder
Fall of Icarus
Musées royaux des Beaux-Arts de Belgique, Brussels

At the National Gallery

What am I to do with these angels' wings,
with the literalness of these gaping heavens
and haloes in the early galleries?
No-one believes them. Beyond meaning,
they are absurd – mannered and posed figures,
as unlikely as the nude's fig-leaf, the wooden
gestures of saints staring straight through you:
uncomfortable attitudes, seeming content
with their fantasies of transfiguration and myth.

Yet the casual visitors walk straight past. They're drawn
to quotidian scenes, the scruffy breeches, old hats
in later pictures, where they scribble notes,
trying to capture the vanishing feelings
of viewing these captured moments of
vanishing things – the recognisable gesture
at an execution, on the river, in the boudoir.
And I with them, yet always end uncomfortably
tracing holiday strolls around Canaletto's
Venice, or impatient somehow with men
who explain to their quiet partners about
dimension, distance, and the need for accuracy.

But Van Gogh's crippled chair confounds them,
restores a sense of things perceived in ways
inconsistent with the camera, eyes jaundiced
only with being human and limited, which is
other than the capture of fleeting things,
the stunned insect, and like verse that must
struggle to avoid its final stop – another fairy-tale,

Gerrit Honthorst
Christ before the High Priest
National Gallery, London

though there are no haloes, no heaven here.
I return to those old pictures, although
I have no theory of art, only a note-book.
Their appeal, uncovered, is the honesty, almost
innocence, time has forced upon them,
for what was then dogma is laughable now, or
almost so. Uncameralike their contentment admits,
rather asserts in all self-consciousness,
other possibilities multiplying beyond the frame:

like the one candle, illuminating a room,
the gleaming table-top, across which one detailed,
serious face confronts another, unnaturally
bound in by a darkness in which we make out
nothing, yet know someone moves, inches beyond
vision, rising, strained forward and demanding:
Give me some light, I say, lights! Now! A taper!

THOMAS HARDY

Christmas in the Elgin Room

British Museum: early last century

'What is the noise that shakes the night,
And seems to soar to the Pole-star height?'
    —'Christmas bells,
    The watchman tells
Who walks this hall that blears us captives with its blight.

'And what, then, mean such clangs, so clear?'
    —''Tis said to have been a day of cheer,
    And source of grace
    To the human race
Long ere their woven sails winged us to exile here.

'We are those whom Christmas overthrew
Some centuries after Pheidias knew
    How to shape us
    And bedrape us
And to set us in Athena's temple for men's view.

'O it is sad now we are sold—
We gods! for Borean people's gold,
    And brought to the gloom
    Of this gaunt room
Which sunlight shuns, and sweet Aurore but enters cold.

Elgin Marbles
British Museum, London

'For all these bells, would I were still
Radiant as on Athenai's Hill.'
　　　—'And I, and I!'
　　　The others sigh,
'Before this Christ was known, and we had men's good will.'

　　　Thereat old Helios could but nod,
　　　Throbbed, too, the Ilissus River-god,
　　　　　and the torsos there
　　　　　Of deities fair,
Whose limbs were shards beneath some Acropolitan clod:

　　　Demeter too, Poseidon hoar,
　　　Persephone, and many more
　　　　　Of Zeus' high breed,—
　　　　　All loth to heed
What the bells sang that night which shook them to the core.

1905 and 1926

Masaccio
The Expulsion
S. Maria del Carmine, Brancacci Chapel, Florence

[24]

Fresco

In Masaccio's 'Expulsion
From the Garden'
how benign the angel seems,
like a good civil servant
he is merely enforcing
the rules. I remember
these faces from Fine Arts 13.
I was young enough then
to think that the loss of innocence
was just about Sex.
Now I see Eve covering
her breasts with her hands
and I know it is not to hide them
but only to keep them
from all she must know
is to follow
from Abel on one,
Cain on the other.

U.A. FANTHORPE

Not my Best Side

I

Not my best side, I'm afraid.
The artist didn't give me a chance to
Pose properly, and as you can see,
Poor chap, he had this obsession with
Triangles, so he left off two of my
Feet. I didn't comment at the time
(What, after all, are two feet
To a monster?) but afterwards
I was sorry for the bad publicity.
Why, I said to myself, should my conqueror
Be so ostentatiously beardless, and ride
A horse with a deformed neck and square hoofs?
Why should my victim be so
Unattractive as to be inedible,
And why should she have me literally
On a string? I don't mind dying
Ritually, since I always rise again,
But I should have liked a little more blood
To show they were taking me seriously.

II

It's hard for a girl to be sure if
She wants to be rescued. I mean, I quite
Took to the dragon. It's nice to be
Liked, if you know what I mean. He was
So nicely physical, with his claws
And lovely green skin, and that sexy tail,
And the way he looked at me,
He made me feel he was all ready to
Eat me. And any girl enjoys that.

Paolo Uccello
St George and the Dragon
National Gallery, London

So when this boy turned up, wearing machinery,
On a really *dangerous* horse, to be honest
I didn't much fancy him. I mean,
What was he like underneath the hardware?
He might have acne, blackheads or even
Bad breath for all I could tell, but the dragon –
Well, you could see all his equipment
At a glance. Still, what could I do?
The dragon got himself beaten by the boy,
And a girl's got to think of her future.

III
I have diplomas in Dragon
Management and Virgin Reclamation.
My horse is the latest model, with
Automatic transmission and built-in
Obsolescence. My spear is custom-built,
And my prototype armour
Still on the secret list. You can't
Do better than me at the moment.
I'm qualified and equipped to the
Eyebrow. So why be difficult?
Don't you want to be killed and/or rescued
In the most contemporary way? Don't
You want to carry out the roles
That sociology and myth have designed for you?
Don't you realise that, by being choosy,
You are endangering job prospects
In the spear- and horse-building industries?
What, in any case, does it matter what
You want? You're in my way.

JON MANCHIP WHITE

The Rout of San Romano

(after the picture by Paolo Uccello)

I watch the battle in the orange-grove
   And wonder who retreated, who advanced,
And why the staid and steady knighthood strove,
   And why the gaudy rocking-horses pranced.

Uccello, somewhat troubled by recession,
   Set the plumed warriors in this flowery place,
And I for one much welcome the digression
   That lends a combat atmosphere and grace.

The vulgar infantry, uncouthly armed,
   Wrestle and run behind with oaths and cries.
The nobles, who infrequently were harmed,
   Engage as cavaliers before my eyes;

A credit to the scroll of chivalry,
   They chase each other in and out the bushes;
The rider with the ivory baton, he,
   In his brocaded mob-cap leads the rushes.

Magnificent his head-dress and his manner,
   Conductor of the antique symphony,
Young Dragon-Casque behind him bears his banner,
   A stiff page holds his helmet on his knee.

And oranges, felicitous motif,
   In verdant clouds meticulously glow,
They bulge with a solicitous relief,
   Refulgent, courtly, painterly they grow.

Paolo Uccello
Rout of San Romano
National Gallery, London

But there, behind, those low-bred rascals scurry,
    Six rogues at butchery upon a hill,
Slower than nightmare must the pikeman hurry,
    And though the screams are numb, they echo still.

Strange how I linger on this far-off highway
    To catch Black Will and Shakebag at their deeds,
While splendid coursers skirmish in the byway,
    A figured dream of which the scholar reads.

O I too sweated, fumbling with a gun:
    I never swung a sword or feutred lance,
In common garb I stumbled on the run
    And grappled coarsely in an awkward stance.

The old knights have my fancy for dominion,
    Yet these half-dozen foot-men have my pity—
Worthless and breathless minion hacks at minion,
    A dirty city sacks a dirty city.

The vagabonds lash out for no fine houses,
    Bestride no chargers with a classic ease,
Rating no ransom, rewarded with carouses,
    Their cadavers will dung the orange-trees.

I know the blackguards for my ancestors.
    Hemmed as we are by rail-and-wire mesh,
The wags anticipate these later wars
    Where crude steel battens cheaply on our flesh.

Well rest you, knights, that struck a blow for beauty,
    You errant, comely crop of hardihood!
God rest you, myrmidons, who did some duty,
    Brothers in blood, a beastly, bitter brood.

ANNE RIDLER

Backgrounds to Italian Paintings: 15th Century

Look between the bow and bowstring, beneath
The flying feet of confederate angels,
Beyond old Montefeltro's triumph seat –
There the delectable landscape lies
Not furtive, but discreet:
It is not hiding, but withholds the secret.
What do the calm foreground figures know of it?
(Suffering martyrdom, riding a triumph
With a crowd of nymphs and Loves about the car)
What do they know of the scenes wherein they are?

The knees of the hills rise from wreaths of sleep,
The distant horsemen glimmer; the pigment fading
Has turned the juniper-green to brown;
And there the river winds away for ever.

Piero della Francesca
Triumph of Montefeltro
Uffizi, Florence

We ourselves have walked those hills and valleys
Where the broom glows and the brittle rock-rose,
Combes are cool with chestnut and plains with poplar:
The juniper there was green – we have been
There, but were not given the secret,
Did not find our rest.

So give this land a stranger's look at best.

Later the landscape stole the picture, the human
Figures were banished, and with the figures vanished
From every natural scene the look of secrets.
So it seems that the figures held the clue.
Gaze at the story boldly as children do –
The wonder awaits you, cornerwise, but never
Full in the face; only the background promises,
Seen through the purple cones at the edge of the eye
And never to be understood:
The sleep-wreathed hills, the ever-winding river.

EZRA POUND

The Picture*

The eyes of this dead lady speak to me,
For here was love, was not to be drowned out.
And here desire, not to be kissed away.
The eyes of this dead lady speak to me.

Of Jacopo del Sellaio

This man knew out the secret ways of love,
No man could paint such things who did not know.
And now she's gone, who was his Cyprian,
And you are here, who are 'The Isles' to me.

And here's the thing that lasts the whole thing out:
The eyes of this dead lady speak to me.

Venus Reclining, by Jacopo del Sellaio (1442–93)

Jacopo del Sellaio
Venus Reclining
National Gallery, London

Soldiers Bathing

The sea at evening moves across the sand.
Under a reddening sky I watch the freedom of a band
Of soldiers who belong to me. Stripped bare
For bathing in the sea, they shout and run in the warm air;
Their flesh, worn by the trade of war, revives
And my mind towards the meaning of it strives.

All's pathos now. The body that was gross,
Rank, ravening, disgusting in the act or in repose,
All fever, filth and sweat, its bestial strength
And bestial decay, by pain and labour grows at length
Fragile and luminous. Poor bare forked animal,
Conscious of his desires and needs and flesh that rise and fall,
Stands in the soft air, tasting after toil
The sweetness of his nakedness: letting the sea-waves coil
Their frothy tongues about his feet, forgets
His hatred of the war, its terrible pressure that begets
That machinery of death and slavery,
Each being a slave and making slaves of others: finds that he
Remembers his proud freedom in a game,
Mocking himself; and comically mimics fear and shame.

Aristotile da Sangallo after Michelangelo
Battle of Cascina Cartoon
Holkham Hall, Norfolk

He plays with death and animality.
And, reading in the shadows of his pallied flesh, I see
The idea of Michelangelo's cartoon
Of soldiers bathing, breaking off before they were half done
At some sortie of the enemy, an episode
Of the Pisan wars with Florence. I remember how he showed
Their muscular limbs that clamber from the water
And heads that turn across the shoulder, eager for the slaughter,
Forgetful of their bodies that are bare
And hot to buckle on and use the weapons lying there.
– And I think too of the theme another found
When, shadowing men's bodies on a sinister red ground –
Was it Uccello or Pollaiuolo? –
Painted a naked battle: warriors, straddled, hacked the foe,
Dug their bare toes into the soil and slew
The brother-naked man who lay between their feet and drew
His lips back from his teeth in a grimace.

They were Italians who knew war's sorrow and disgrace
And showed the thing suspended, stripped. A theme
Born out of the experience of that horrible extreme
Of war beneath a sky where the air flows
With *Lachrimae Christi*. For that rage, that bitterness, those
     blows
That hatred of the slain, what could it be
But indirectly or directly a commentary
On the Crucifixion? and the picture burns
With indignation and pity and despair by turns
Because it is the obverse of the scene
Where Christ hangs murdered, stripped, upon the Cross.
    I mean,
That is the explanation of its rage.

And we too have our bitterness and pity that engage
Blood, spirit in this war. But night begins,
Night of the mind: who nowadays is conscious of our sins?
Though every human deed concerns our blood,
And even we must know what nobody has understood,
That some great love is over all we do
And that is what has driven us to fury, for so few
Can suffer all the terror of that love:
The terror of that love has set us spinning in this groove
Greasy with our blood.
                              These dry themselves and dress,
Resume their shirts, forget the fright and shame of
        nakedness.
Because to love is terrible we prefer
The freedom of our crimes; yet, as I drink the dusky air,
I feel a strange delight that fills me full,
Strange gratitude, as if evil itself were beautiful,
And kiss the wound in thought, while in the west
I watch a streak of red that might have issued from Christ's
        breast.

R.S. THOMAS

Threshold

I emerge from the mind's
cave into the worse darkness
outside, where things pass and
the Lord is in none of them.

I have heard the still, small voice
and it was that of the bacteria
demolishing my cosmos. I
have lingered too long on

this threshold, but where can I go?
To look back is to lose the soul
I was leading upward towards
the light. To look forward? Ah,

what balance is needed at
the edges of such an abyss.
I am alone on the surface
of a turning planet. What

to do but, like Michelangelo's
Adam, put my hand
out into unknown space,
hoping for the reciprocating touch?

Michelangelo
Creation of Adam
Sistine Chapel, Rome

DANNIE ABSE

Crepuscolo

*Crepuscolo (Evening) is one of the partly finished statues by
Michelangelo in the Medici Chapel, San Lorenzo.*

To the grey Sacristy of San Lorenzo
tourists come whispering lest they waken
this self-absorbed statue and it assail
each prying one of them, lest a stone hand
uplift to point and the stone head utter,
slowly turning, 'Wrongdoing and shame prevail!'

Once all drowsy in Carrara. Harmlessly,
unnumbered shadows brooded under the weight
of rock-ledges, lizards hardly animate.
Then certain men came. Still the stone's cry
safe and soundless, still the statue slumbered
in the refuge of the rock's estate.

But, soon, massive slabs were brutally urged
from the mountain – the half-bright, half-stripped bodies
of workmen struggling in dazzle and bone-
white powder of marble, smoking sunlight.
How could they discern the one waking there
or hear stone words in the larynx of the stone?

And later, in Florence? Only the sculptor
heard the statue, almost delivered, crying
'Dear to me is sleep, dearer to be at peace,
in stone, while wrongdoing and shame prevail.
Not to see, not to know, would be a great blessing.'
So the statue pleaded, so the sculptor ceased.

More than four hundred years since they set out
from Carrara, each mile cursed and supervised.
The body in the rock staying young but the hair
turning grey and the face aging utterly –
its idioplasm fixed, its night-accepting look
despairingly defined in the eyes not there.

Now, this evening, on exercise, three warplanes
dive on Carrara, flee, return, rehearse
radioactive speeeds so shamelessly
that, in the x-rayed mountain, another
fifty million statues cower, unhatched,
and not one, stone-enslaved, wanting to be free.

Michelangelo
Crepuscolo
S. Lorenzo, Medici Chapel, Florence

WILLIAM CARLOS WILLIAMS

The Dance

In Brueghel's great picture, The Kermess,
the dancers go round, they go round and
around, the squeal and the blare and the
tweedle of bagpipes, a bugle and fiddles
tipping their bellies (round as the thick-
sided glasses whose wash they impound)
their hips and their bellies off balance
to turn them. Kicking and rolling about
the Fair Grounds, swinging their butts, those
shanks must be sound to bear up under such
rollicking measures, prance as they dance
in Brueghel's great picture, The Kermess.

Pieter Brueghel the Elder
Peasant Dance
Kunsthistorisches Museum, Vienna

PETER PORTER

Looking at a Melozzo da Forlì

And in this instance we think of you, God,
You beard above all things,
Canceller of every fact except death,
Looking down on your grand intercession,
Orthodox, like the artist's vision,
Helpless helper of time and promise.

But we do not get closer to love.
The angel's admonitory finger
And the lily of greeting tell Mary only
That the clock in her womb is ticking,
That she will come sooner to sorrow.

And I can see too in the structures
Of church and family another death.
We are entered by the spirit
And thereafter comes such rich despair –
Sermons of the penis, oddities by the seashore
Where towns have sunk, letters lost
In the mumblings of a drunken alphabet.

What is Mary kneeling on? A yoke,
A box for Miss Plath's mad bees,
A stiff pew for a Protestant Sunday?
In one revolution her body shows
Disquiet, reflection, inquiry, submission, merit.

These shapes Melozzo put on a wall
Fade like the dove-voiced poet
Into a high wood of darkness.
From his flat-bottomed cloud, God observes
Earthly love and sadness, saying
After all, this is only a language of gestures.

Yes Mary, you are an actor in a play
Whose dénouement is now to be spoken.
I rehearse the lines myself to your angel –
The action is beginning, blessèd is the Virgin
Who shall be the mother of death.

Melozzo da Forli
Annunciation
Pantheon, Rome

THOM GUNN

In Santa Maria del Popolo

Waiting for when the sun an hour or less
Conveniently oblique makes visible
The painting on one wall of this recess
By Caravaggio, of the Roman School,
I see how shadow in the painting brims
With a real shadow, drowning all shapes out
But a dim horse's haunch and various limbs,
Until the very subject is in doubt.

But evening gives the act, beneath the horse
And one indifferent groom, I see him sprawl,
Forshortened from the head, with hidden face,
Where he has fallen, Saul becoming Paul.
O wily painter, limiting the scene
From a cacophony of dusty forms
To the one convulsion, what is it you mean
In that wide gesture of the lifting arms?

No Ananias croons a mystery yet,
Casting the pain out under name of sin.
The painter saw what was, an alternate
Candour and secrecy inside the skin.
He painted, elsewhere, that firm insolent
Young whore in Venus' clothes, those pudgy cheats,
Those sharpers; and was strangled, as things went,
For money, by one such picked off the streets.

I turn, hardly enlightened, from the chapel
To the dim interior of the church instead,
In which there kneel already several people,
Mostly old women: each head closeted

In tiny fists holds comfort as it can.
Their poor arms are too tired for more than this
– For the large gesture of solitary man,
Resisting, by embracing, nothingness.

Caravaggio
Conversion of St Paul
S. Maria del Popolo, Cerasi Chapel, Rome

DAVID WRIGHT

By the Effigy of St Cecilia

Having peculiar reverence for this creature
Of the numinous imagination, I am come
To visit her church and stand before the altar
Where her image, hewn in pathetic stone,
Exhibits the handiwork of her executioner.

There are the axemarks. Outside, in the courtyard,
In shabby habit, an Italian nun
Came up and spoke: I had to answer, 'Sordo.'
She said she was a teacher of deaf children
And had experience of my disorder.

And I have had experience of her order,
Interpenetrating chords and marshalled sound;
Often I loved to listen to the organ's
Harmonious and concordant interpretation
Of what is due from us to the creation.

But it was taken from me in my childhood
And those graduated pipes turned into stone.
Now, having travelled a long way through silence,
Within the church in Trastevere I stand
A pilgrim to the patron saint of music

And am abashed by the presence of this nun
Beside the embodiment of that legendary
Virgin whose music and whose martyrdom
Is special to this place: by her reality.
She is a reminder of practical kindness,

The care it takes to draw speech from the dumb
Or pierce with sense the carapace of deafness;
And so, of the plain humility of the ethos
That constructed, also, this elaborate room
To pray for bread in; they are not contradictory.

Stefano Maderno
St Cecilia
Church of St Cecilia, Rome

EDWARD LUCIE-SMITH

Rubens to Hélène Fourment

Now sinking towards age, I paint your rising.
Your flesh grows with my sunset. You wrap close
A dark fur robe, which clothes and half unclothes
   you.
Each little movement brushes the rich texture
Against thigh, buttocks, breast. And now I serve
More fiercely than I did our wedding night
Your pearly substance. Dear, I know too well
What you in your turn see: a florid statesman
Burdened with excess of fame. If the long years
Instruct me now in fusing tone with tone
Until the painted you seems made of flowers,
My skill is nothing to you, just the years.

                  You bring a sort of love
To meet my love. I know that all I've taught
Your lovely body in our linen sheets
Would run at once to meet me if I touched you.
But when I go? – I see you plan already.
Good Flemish thoughts stir in those aqueous eyes
Of what a rich young widow, fertile (see
The proof of healthy children) can expect.
Whom will you choose to reap my benefits?
A noble? Young? A warrior? Look, Hélène –
My pictures give a blessing. The dark steel
A hero's clad in many a time reflects
Like bonfires in its depth, the rosy sheen
Of woman armoured just as you are now.

                  And yet I win:

I paint this picture. No-one will remember
Another man has owned you. Everyone
Will see you thus, in the act of being possessed
More coarsely, more completely than in all
The many separate times I came to take you.

I chose well. And I chose. It was not folly,
A doddering, mumbling, stupid lickerishness,
Made me pick you. I might have married nobly,
But nothing so noble as this youthful body.
I find more meaning here than I've discovered
In all the allegories my patrons set me.
My lust cried for you. But love, too, for the race,
The female richness. I can hardly tell
Sometimes on waking whether I have dreamt
Of walking slowly near my tower of Steen
The fields I own, the hedge-paths, or if I
Have simply strolled about that rich estate
Hélène's young body. Why do these, the blue
Veins by your neck, the lesser pearls
Circling the large pearl in your flowering nipples,
Even the feet, cramped by fine shoes I gave you,
Seem more like landmarks than the marks we set
To show where Steen's fields march beside a neighbour's?
I feed upon you, warm my hands before you,
You ward the rains off, bring me government
(The hand governs the brush, the mind the hand,
The mind's discipline is to recreate you).
Your flesh springs from that dark robe like a rainbow
Bursting a cloud, and is as full of promise.

Rubens
La Pélisse
Kunsthistorisches Museum, Vienna

Sometimes, these nights, a wild hunt fills my dream:
A lioness, impaled, that tries to reach me
Up my stout spear-shaft. Then the highly-pitched clamour
Of fallen men and claw-raked stallions screaming
Is muted to a buzz, and leaning down
Out of the saddle as my horse rears skyward
I see, moving small and clear within the tawny
Crystal of eyes, your double image – silks
And golden tresses, And I wake to find
You move beneath me like a lioness,
Silken and supple, naked in our bed,
Face veiled beneath a golden fall of hair.

I pass you on in entail. They inherit
Who learn to look. I leave you to be hunted
By other appetites. I cannot help
But bring my nature to your natural good.
I set all down, and sign you: RUBENS PINXIT.

THEODORE WEISS

Ten Little Rembrandts

There, with ten Rembrandts
or so, he slumped in the corner
like a sloppy janitor, an ex-sexton
in a corner of heaven, one eye opening
to say with a sigh as the bustle
flutters by him: 'God again!'

So you speak with uneasy,
loving regret of Paris: 'I do love it
but never feel comfortable in it.
And this time I gave it ten days.
But then the Parisians don't seem
much at home in it either. The Louvre

with its ages on ages
of dust, rooms empty, and the room
with ten little Rembrandts, and that
crumpled old guard snoring away
in one corner! Well, I flew back
home soon after, and almost at once

the whole trip, the pictures,
the operas, the plays, the cities,
became little more than a point
in time. But I assure myself
that each did something, is doing
now, and will go on doing. Who knows.'

And you remind me of another
brooding on the Brooklyn lectures,
one in particular of a famous writer,
she heard in her youth: 'A Russ
he might have been, enflamed
about the havoc that had plagued

his world, its scars long
after visible, about the dead
there seemed not earth, not mind
and time, enough to bury. But I can't
remember anything any more. No, not
the speaker's name or even some

one quirk he may have had.
But I keep hoping that all that
got into me and is working still.'
All that, like ten little Rembrandts
hard at work, in the mighty space
of our forgetting exerting wily wills.

Rembrandt
Scholar in his Study
Louvre, Paris

EARLE BIRNEY

El Greco: Espolio

The carpenter is intent on the pressure of his hand
on the awl, and the trick of pinpointing his strength
through the awl to the wood, which is tough.
He has no effort to spare for despoilings
nor to worry if he'll be cut in on the dice.
His skill is vital to the scene, and the safety of the state.
Anyone can perform the indignities; it is his hard arms
and craft that hold the eyes of the convict's women.
There is the problem of getting the holes straight
(in the middle of this shoving crowd)
and deep enough to hold the spikes
after they've sunk through those soft feet
and wrists waiting behind him.

The carpenter isn't aware that one of the hands
is held in a curious beseechment over him –
but what is besought, forgiveness or blessing? –
nor if he saw would he take the time to be puzzled.
Criminals come in all sorts, as anyone knows who makes crosses,
are as mad or sane as those who decide on their killings.
Our one at least has been quiet so far
though they say he has talked himself into this trouble –
a carpenter's son who got notions of preaching.
Well here's a carpenter's son who'll have carpenter's sons,
God willing, and build what's wanted, temples or tables,
mangers or crosses, and shape them decently,
working alone in that firm and profound abstraction
which blots out the bawling of rag-snatchers.
To construct with hands, knee-weight, braced thigh,
keeps the back turned from death.
But it's too late now for the other carpenter's boy
to return to this peace before the nails are hammered.

El Greco
Espolio
National Trust, Upton House

SEAMUS HEANEY

Summer 1969

While the Constabulary covered the mob
Firing into the Falls, I was suffering
Only the bullying sun of Madrid.
Each afternoon, in the casserole heat
Of the flat, as I sweated my way through
The life of Joyce, stinks from the fishmarket
Rose like the reek off a flax-dam.
At night on the balcony, gules of wine,
A sense of children in their dark corners,
Old women in black shawls near open windows,
The air a canyon rivering in Spanish.
We talked our way home over starlit plains
Where patent leather of the Guardia Civil
Gleamed like fish-bellies in flax-poisoned waters.

'Go back,' one said, 'try to touch the people.'
Another conjured Lorca from his hill.
We sat through death counts and bullfight reports
On the television, celebrities
Arrived from where the real thing still happened.

I retreated to the cool of the Prado.
Goya's 'Shooting of the Third of May'
Covered a wall – the thrown-up arms
And spasm of the rebel, the helmeted
And knapsacked military, the efficient
Rake of the fusillade. In the next room
His nightmares, grafted to the palace wall –
Dark cyclones, hosting, breaking; Saturn
Jewelled in the blood of his own children,
Gigantic Chaos turning his brute hips
Over the world. Also, that holmgang
Where two berserks club each other to death
For honour's sake, greaved in a bog, and sinking.

He painted with his fists and elbows, flourished
The stained cape of his heart as history charged.

Goya
Panic
Prado, Madrid

STEVIE SMITH

Spanish School

The painters of Spain
Dipped their brushes in pain
By grief on a gallipot
Was Spanish tint begot.

Just see how Theotocopoulos
Throws on his canvas
Colours of hell
Christ lifts his head to cry
Once more I bleed and die
Mary emaciated cries:
Are men not satiated?
Must the blood of my son
For ever run?
The sky turns to burning oil
Blood red and yellow boil
Down from on high
Will no hills fall on us
To hide the sky?
Y Luciente's pen
Traces the life of men
Christs crucified upon a slope
They have no hope
Like Calderon who wrote in grief and scorn:

The greatest crime of man's to have been born.
Dr Péral
In a coat of gray
Has a way
With his mouth which seems to say
A lot
But nothing very good to hear
And as for Doña Ysabel Corbos de Porcel
Well
What a bitch
This seems to me a portrait which
Might have been left unhung
Or at anyrate slung
A little higher up.

But never mind there's always Ribera
With his little lamb
(Number two-four-four)
To give a more
Genial atmosphere
And a little jam
For the pill –
But still.

PART II

FROM STUBBS TO SEURAT

EDWARD LUCIE-SMITH

On Looking at Stubbs's
'Anatomy of the Horse'

In Lincolnshire, a village full of tongues
Not tired by a year's wagging, and a man
Shut in a room where a wrecked carcass hangs,
His calm knife peeling putrid flesh from bone.
He whistles softly, as an ostler would;
The dead horse moves, as if it understood.

That night a yokel holds the taproom still
With tales new-hatched; he's peeped, and seen a mare
Stand there alive with naked rib and skull –
The creature neighed, and stamped upon the floor;
The warlock asked her questions, and she spoke;
He wrote her answers down in a huge book.

Two centuries gone, I have the folio here,
And turn the pages, find them pitiless.
These charts of sinew, vein and bone require
A glance more expert, more detached than this –
Fingering the margins, I think of the old
Sway-backed and broken nags the pictures killed.

Yet, standing in that room, I watch the knife;
Light dances on it as it maps a joint
Or scribes a muscle; I am blank and stiff
The blade cuts so directly to my want;
I gape for anecdote, absurd detail,
Like any yokel with his pint of ale.

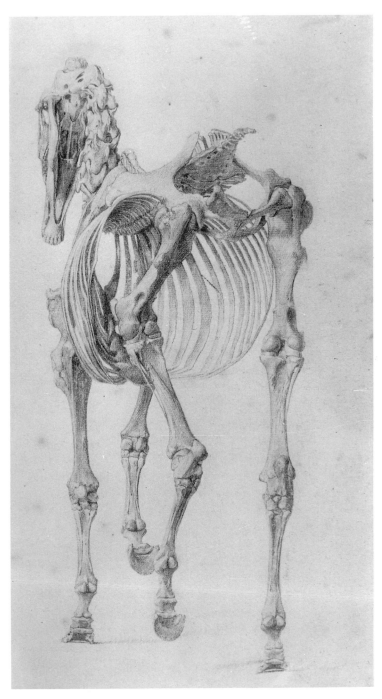

George Stubbs
Anatomy of the Horse
Royal Academy of Arts, London

DANIEL HOFFMAN

from

Brotherly Love

Always a rush of interest in the painting of Penn's Treaty
Whenever Penn's country is at war,
In 1941 Penn's Treaty on each card in decks of playing cards,
On Provident Insurance Company calendars and in the Bulletin of the
    Friends
Historical Association, in ads in *Newsweek*, *Time*
And full-color in encyclopaedias printed despite the shortages of war,
Since then, the country constantly at war, West's Treaty reappearing
In books on history, on painting, and on Benjamin West,
On Quakers, Pennsylvania, Christianity in the United States,
In *Our Heritage*, *Landmarks of Liberty*, *Corse di Storia*
E di Educazione Civica (in Rome), in books in Sweden,
    Germany, England of course, and France,
Made into slides for the National Gallery and the Metropolitan Museum,
Reproduced in *Klein Schriften zu Kunst, Literatur, Philosophie,*
    Geschichte und Politik,
And *The American Heritage History of the United States,*
Shown on TV, the paintings of the painting and the copies
In litho or engraving, book or magazine
All collectible and valued at a price, some even beyond price,
West's original, for instance, long shown in Independence Hall,
Now at the Pennsylvania Academy of Fine Arts, where thousands see it,
many sending an image of its image
On color postcards home –
But few, how few, of those who've pondered the Great Peace-Maker
And his stolid Quakers and the Indian chief and sachems
And the lithe-limbed Indian mother with her babe sucking her breast
Or fingers, how few have ever read or even wondered
What, exactly what, in truth, was promised and agreed to,
Deliberated and palavered, signed and the Peace-Pipe smoked on
– I mean the text, that tells who gave, who got
How much for what at Shackamaxon
in Penn's Treaty with the Indians?

Benjamin West
Penn's Treaty with the Indians
Pennsylvania Academy of the Fine Arts, Philadelphia

Joseph Wright of Derby
Sir Brooke Boothby
Tate Gallery, London

Sir Brooke Boothby

Sir Brooke, reclining by a brook,
How punningly your lines flow
Beside your namesake. Time has changed
The leaves to autumn overhead.
You clasp Rousseau.

And all your nature's heraldry
Is here set out. It is your look –
Voluptuous, thoughtful, quizzical,
Has puzzled me for many years,
Beloved Sir Brooke.

Two years ago they cleaned you up.
Still sensuous, you leer the less,
No longer the seducer but
Hinting of sorrows yet to come,
And pensiveness.

Yet still amused, – you scrutinise
Me as intently as I you.
Dumpy and old, I've fared the worse.
Will others come when I am gone,
Or be as true?

My very sparkling Brooke, we are
Two centuries and Styx apart.
Yet mirror-imaged our loss
(Your child, my father) and we share
A love for art.

It would be pleasant if we were
Among the leaves so juxtaposed –
You on the left, I on the right –
That you would flow above me when
The book was closed.

JONATHAN PRICE

Experiment with an Air Pump
by Joseph Wright 'of Derby'

He made a work of art out of suffocation:
While the bird in the thinning air gasps, dies,
Some chat, a soft-hearted girl covers her eyes,
Others calmly observe the demonstration;

A low-set candle provides dramatic lighting.
It doesn't look the same under sixty watts
After a typical day; but there are lots
Of people like oneself going down fighting

For the last time, fighting for the last breath.
Nobody paints them. Their husbands or their wives
Notice the difference as they work out their lives
Committed to each other and to death.

Joseph Wright of Derby
Experiment with an Air-Pump
National Gallery, London

Sir Henry Raeburn
Rev. Robert Walker Skating on Duddingston Loch
National Galleries of Scotland, Edinburgh

JAMES AITCHISON

Uncertain Grace

*After Raeburn's 'The Reverend Robert Walker
Skating On Duddingston Loch', painted in 1784*

Backwards
the world wobbles and tilts
backwards
with the tottering half-steps.

A timorous first thrust
and the impetus takes him out across the ice:
decorously maladroit,
he semaphores genteel alarm
as he glides in an uncontrollable glissade
ungainly from the safety of the shore
into the ambivalence
of body's lightness and unbearable bulk.

He thrusts again,
lets go his trembling hold on nothingness
and rediscovers the uncertain grace
of skating through a Monday afternoon
alone on frozen Duddingston Loch.

Iron and ice release
a sweeter music than yesterday's psalms,
and the effortless inscription of these rings
round and round the centre of the loch
is more persuasive than any sermon.

That huddle of wintering greylag on the edge
is an appropriate congregation
for this illicit sacrament.
For the other flock would surely disapprove
of all these circles
and the absence of straight lines.

Oh, yes, the people fear their God,
whoever that may be,
but they fear each other more, much more.
And locked in their frozen souls there lies
an inadmissible fear
like some enormous secret that drives out
all the little foolish tender things.

Yesterday's communion services –
with whom or what did they commune
in that mood of cold idolatry
in the crowded Canongate Kirk? –
were dress rehearsals for the Judgement Day,
for the sure and certain grace of Almighty God.
Such ice might crack, perhaps, but never melt.

He really must abandon the hope
of preaching a cycle of perfect sermons
from First Corinthians;
how absurd the notion seems now
on a day of skating, in an age of ice.

Pray instead for this abandonment
of body and mind adrift
in awkward elegance on the frozen loch;
pray that there be time and ice enough
to skate again in this uncertain grace.

D. J. ENRIGHT

God Creating Adam

Either He is fatigued –
Creation takes it out of you
And this is the sixth day –
Or else He is having second thoughts.
(But God's first are always right.)

Adam has no thoughts at the moment,
Only a certain bewilderment:
It was all so sudden,
There's no substitute for a leisurely womb.

He hardly seems a sufficient abyss
To be so intensely brooded over.
How can he hope to live up to it?

The serpent is already coiled about him.
Surely a premature appearance?
(Though no surprise to the Omniscient.)

Heretics would say later, it was life
Snaking out of Adam's right foot –
As if He'd left a hole in it!
Or perhaps intended, Eve as yet undreamt of,
For a household pet. Snakes have clean habits.

Prudently God provides Adam with ribs in plenty:
No need to start from scratch next time.
'I must create a system,' He is thinking,
'And leave the rest to them . . .'
The snake is whispering about a thing called 'sex',
Though what it is he doesn't know from Adam.

[77]

Can that really be the sunset –
Louring and chaotic?
It doesn't look natural,
Not exactly the shepherd's delight.

Next there would have to be a Shepherd.
That's the trouble with creating,
There's no end to it.

William Blake
Elohim Creating Adam
Tate Gallery, London

JOHN WAIN

J.M.W. Turner: 'The Shipwreck'

This canvas yells the fury of the sea.
Across a quiet room, where people murmur
their poised appreciations, it shrieks out
the madness of the wind.
                                    How can that be?
Woven of voiceless threads, its pigments laid
with 'no more sound than the mice make', it hurls
the tempest at my eardrums, and my eyes
smart in the lashing spray. But not before
the colours of tragedy have enkindled them:
it must be so, because the colours hold
the secret. They are noise, and tilt, and steepness.
The colours are trough, and crash, the cry of gulls
lifted and blown away like part of the spume.
The colours are the bawling of the wind.
That yellow sail, its mast snapped sideways, catches
into itself and holds that gleam of light
amid the livid waters, the evening gleam
through torn black cloud as the sullen day departs.
One last message of life. Over and out.
The people in the small escaping boat
(too frail for the uncaring slide and smash
of those tall water-cliffs, promising only
ten minutes more of life, of clinging on
before the toppling plunge) see in that yellow
the last of life that they will ever see.
A goodbye signal, perhaps a welcoming
to those new neighbours, whoever they will be,
who wait for them on the other side of darkness,
below the clap of the waves and lace of foam
down there in the dark, and then below the dark,
in the calm of the still depths (the most tremendous
storm makes no disturbance below nine fathoms).
Will their new world be down on the ocean-floor,
among the caves? Or, following the blown gulls,

J.M.W. Turner
The Shipwreck
Tate Gallery, London

through some still gleaming crevice of the sky?
Or will they start again on the green earth,
as newts this time, or leaning-tower giraffes,
or crocodiles who lie still as old tyres
in estuary mud? Or human children
with different facial bones and frizzy hair?
Or will they be the atoms of the water
next time, and hammer some trim ketch to planks
and floating spars? Will they be starfish, lying
five-pointed on the beach these voyagers
would give, in this death-minute, everything
they ever owned to be treading, calmly, now?
Who knows? What we can ask, I think, is
whether death will seem beautiful to them when it comes,
and to us, for that matter, after the pain
is over, I mean. Many great artists have
extolled the beauty of death, have loved and called to it,
and Turner here seems to be saying *Now*
I will show you how terror and agony
and the utterly final arrival of death can distil
an essence of beauty-in-terror, an enrichment
in the moment of final relinquishment of all:
as if it took that knowledge, that edge of torment,
to peel away the cataract from our vision,
to reveal the beauty of those mad waters
and that last gleam of light from a hostile day.
Meanwhile, one thing I know: the silent canvas
has stored the howl and thunder of that hour,
the yell of death in the ears of the sacrificed:
the last groan of the timbers, the frantic slap
of the saturated sail. Canvas to canvas. Sound
to silence, through the artist's compassionate mind,
and back to sound again, as I stand here.
Oh, it has 'painterly values' too, and can be discussed
in purely abstract terms: but not now, not now.
Some other time, not in the presence of
the human creatures, air-breathers, gulping their last,
and the sea's roaring that never will be quenched,
and beyond, the starfish at his supine vigil
on the final beach whose shingle we shall be.

B.C. LEALE

Sketch by Constable

The dog knows it's an early draft. He's
full of destinations and joy as he
rounds the first bend from the house –
his shadow sharp, vibrant. Even the
path's edge is of frisky earth.

About five years later he's finished.
His short run by the water's edge completed and
he's famous. With muted shadow he looks up
to the men in a motionless hay-wain.

John Constable
Willy Lott's House near Flatford Mill
Victoria and Albert Museum, London

A Reproduction of Constable's
'Salisbury Cathedral' in a Room on a Greek Island

For a moment, time and motion stop still:
Shadows are lengthening across the meadow,
Evensong voices collect together and fling
Jerusalem into the vast cathedral space;
An English summer evening is coming to a close.

Beyond the slit window, the wall
Extends to beat off the scorch.
Flies dizzy the naked light bulb;
One flies too low and a hand flicks out
With the autonomy of a donkey's tail.

At the wood-dark water of the stream
Emerging half-highlighted in the shade,
A cow, her burnished anvil-boned backside
Anchored on the bank, has raised her head
And lets water drool out of her mouth.

Here, airless heat dries the skin.
Whitewash thinly bruises the plaster,
Nylon mesh curtains are strung up
Like chickens in ragged weightlessness.
Drawers are parched with yellow newspaper.

On the path, a man with a hat and frock coat
Points his cane. His idle remarks are unanswered
By the bonneted lady, draped in scarlet,
Standing out from the greeny golden cascade
Of foliage like a bird of paradise.

There is dust under the jammed tap.
A cracked glass is flaked with toothpaste;
A cockroach glistens black in the corner,
The air is as hot as exhaled breath,
The bare walls are closing in.

Through the arching elms, towards the clouds,
The cathedral rises. The service is ending –
'I shall not cease from mental fight' –
While the light settles on the mitre-shaped windows
The stony buttresses preserving stability.

What great lodestone must exist to draw up
This great spire and the smaller ones frosted on
Like stalagmites, and uplift the spirit
From the despondency of the earthbound body
Into the coolness of England's green and pleasant land?

John Constable
Salisbury Cathedral; from the Bishop's Grounds
Victoria and Albert Museum, London

JOHN ASH

Poor Boy: Portrait of a Painting

Difficult to say what all of this is all about.
Being young. Or simply arrogance, lack of patience –

a misunderstanding about what the word maturity
can mean when exchanged among 'real' adults . . .

I don't know what kind of plant that is, but it
is green and has a small red flower

and the glass it strives towards is latticed,
yellowish and cracked. Beyond it

roofs are bunched together like boats
in a popular harbour
and through it the inevitable light falls . . .

And the light is art! It is arranged *so*,
over the bed and the pale dead boy,
his astonishing red hair, the shirt rumpled like sculpture,

the breeches. . . . The breeches are a problem:
no one can decide whether they are blue
or mauve. Versions differ. But the light

is faultless. It can hit anything
whatever the distance –
for example, the squashed triangle of white lining
to the stiff, mulberry coloured dressing-gown,
the torn-up sheets of poems or pornography,
the oriental blade of pallor above
the boy's large, left eye-lid or even the small, brown
dope bottle lying on the scrubbed floor
almost at the bottom of the picture. Of course

much depends on the angle. Much remains
obscure, but this only enhances
these significant islands of brilliance,

exposed and absolutely
vulnerable to our interpretation:

there is nowhere he can hide the hand that rests
just above his stomach as if he still felt horribly ill.

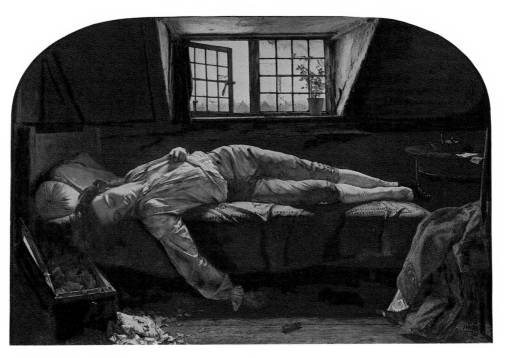

Henry Wallis
Chatterton
Tate Gallery, London

JOHN ORMOND

Certain Questions for Monsieur Renoir

Did you then celebrate
That grave discovered blue
With salt thrown on a fire
In honour of all blues?

I mean the dress of La Parisienne
(Humanly on the verge of the ceramic),
Blue of Delft, dream summary of blues,
Centre-piece of a fateful exhibition;

Whose dress-maker and, for that matter,
Stays-maker the critics scorned;
Who every day receives her visitors
In my country where the hard slate is blue.

She has been dead now nearly a century
Who wears that blue of smoke curling
Beyond a kiln, and blue of gentians,
Blue of lazurite, turquoise hauled

Over the blue waves, blue water, from Mount Sinai;
Clematis blue: she, Madame Henriot,
Whose papers fall to pieces in the files
In the vaults of the Registrar General.

Did you see in her garment the King of Illyria
Naming his person's flower in self-love?
And in the folds, part of polyphony
Of all colour, thunder blue,

Blue of blue slipper-clay, blue
Of the blue albatross? Blue sometimes
Without edge, blue liquified
By distance? Or did they start

Auguste Renoir
La Parisienne
National Museum of Wales, Cardiff

Those ribbons at her wrists in blue
Of a sea-starwort? Or in verdigris, perhaps,
Blue on a Roman bead? Or in that regal blue
Of the Phœnicians, of boiled whelks;

That humbly-begun but conquering blue
Which, glowing, makes a god of man?
She who is always poised between appointments
For flirtation, what nuances of blue

Her bodice had, this blue you made
For your amusement, painter of fans and porcelain,
You set on gaiety; who saw, in the blue fog
Of the city, a candle burning blue

(Not heralding a death but) harbouring
A clear illusion, blue spot on the young salmon,
A greater blue in shadow; blue's calm
Insistence on a sense. Not for you

Indigo blue, or blue of mummy's cloth
Or the cold unction of mercury's blue ointment,
But the elect blue of love in constancy,
Blue, true blue; blue gage, blue plum,

Blue fibrils of a form, roundness
Absorbed by light, quintessence
Of blue beautiful. It was not blue
Tainted, taunted by dark. Confirm it.

The eyes are bells to blue
Inanimate pigment set alight
By gazing which was passionate.
So what is midnight to this midinette?

Ultramarine, deep-water blue?
Part of a pain and darkness never felt?
Assyrian crystal? Clouded blue malachite?

Blue of a blue dawn trusting light.

D.J. ENRIGHT

Home and Colonial

Henri Rousseau's 'Tropical Storm with Tiger'

I'm not one of those simpletons who believe
That if only they had a larger TV screen
They would be able to see the naughty bits.
But if that picture were a few inches longer,
Here on the right-hand side, I mean – then
In fact you would see – not a naughty bit –
You would see me.

Sexual behaviour does exist in the tropics –
Oh indeed – but it's relatively invisible.
It doesn't go on in public. And it wouldn't
Even if there weren't a storm, even if
The jungle weren't so full of spiky things.

Public sex is less sex than public, I reckon.
Like that young couple in the Underground
The other night. They weren't doing anything,
They were simulating it. In my day
We used to dissimulate. And likewise I doubt
This notion that a wider screen creates
A broader mind. What you can see is never
The interesting part. Though of course
I'm not referring to a gentleman like you
Looking at a picture like this
In a reputable gallery.

Imagination is allowed some latitude,
I know (though, as it happens, this painting
Doesn't get enough), but all the same . . .

Henri Rousseau
Tropical Storm with Tiger
National Gallery, London

The jungle is not as pretty as it looks here,
Untidy at the best, storm or no storm.
The bougainvillaea was tatty and blotched,
Not right out of a hothouse. It was gloomy –
That's another thing about jungles – and
The lightning had that lost air it always has
In those parts. Fumbling around for something
To get a grip on, like a roof, a chimney
Or a golf-club.

But the tiger – Frenchy's hit it off to a T!
Scared stiff, what with its tail behind, which it
Took for a flying snake, and in front – a hairy
Red-faced white man in a post-impressionist sarong,
Heading for the nearest drinking shop.
I fancied an ice-cold Guinness. A moment later
And there'd have been just me on that canvas,
Dry and wet at once, sarong slipping a bit,
Tiger a mile away and still running.

Even so, would you really see more on a larger screen,
D'you think? Or do the girls wear towels or something?

RICHARD WILBUR

Museum Piece

The good grey guardians of art
Patrol the halls on spongy shoes,
Impartially protective, though
Perhaps suspicious of Toulouse.

Here dozes one against the wall,
Disposed upon a funeral chair.
A Degas dancer pirouettes
Upon the parting of his hair.

See how she spins! The grace is there,
But strain as well is plain to see.
Degas loved the two together:
Beauty joined to energy.

Edgar Degas purchased once
A fine El Greco, which he kept
Against the wall beside his bed
To hang his pants on while he slept.

Edgar Degas
Two Dancers on the Stage
Courtauld Institute Galleries, London
(Courtauld Collection)

DANNIE ABSE

At The Tate

If the dead owned ears that refused to crumble
perhaps they would hear one sound for ever
from yesterday or patient years ago:
either the bellowing in the crematorium
or the earth rumbling down on the coffin.
'La vie, cette merveille', cried Rodin, but the dead
accuse Creation, resemble stone.
This dolorous thought first, then the sculpture,
the embodiment of an illusion.
Shoes squeaking, autumn sunlight, parquet floors,
as Rodin's lovers keep on kissing
and not kissing. These statues are listening
not to their own heartbeats, erotic sighs,
immoderate, endearing promises,
nor to knowing voices: 'How Rodin praised Life!'
Rather they hear, if they hear at all,
always and haunted, between intervals
of a silence that is not the silence here,
one man's exhalations of discontent –
the sculptor muttering. 'Toujours travailler,'
and, blow after blow, the noise of hammer
on chisel, the protracted cry of surfaces.
Most statues seem sad and introspective,
they hold their breath between coming and going,
they lament their devoured, once shuddering stone.

Auguste Rodin
The Kiss
Tate Gallery, London

Vincent Van Gogh
Portrait of the Artist's Mother
The Norton Simon Art Foundation,
Pasadena, California

ROBERT FAGLES

Portrait of the Artist's Mother

Photography, demon of reproduction – I despise it.
So black-and-white, this tintype of mother,
unbearable.
                    Too reminiscent of the past,
the rift within herself: part love, part dogma,
starched as a nun in the parsonage at Etten.
Reminiscent of the growing rift between us –
how she clings to the life hereafter,
clings to the first Vincent,
the infant dead, my double, my accuser.

Mother, you are so distant
I will paint you with a vengeance,
draw you from memory . . .
                              three years gone,
1,000 kilometers out of Holland,
south beneath this sun – and all I see
is violet, somber, blossoming into yellow,
strict lips
        glistening into a smile
                    your brow expansive, blond.

Of the life hereafter I know nothing, mother,
but when I paint you what I feel is yellow,
lemon yellow, the halo of the rose.

Toulouse Lautrec at the Moulin Rouge

'Cognac – more cognac for Monsieur Lautrec –
More cognac for the little gentleman,
Monster or clown of the Moulin – quick –
Another glass!'
                  The Can Can
Chorus with their jet net stockings
And their red heads rocking
Have brought their patrons flocking to the floor.
Pince-nez, glancing down from legs advancing
To five fingers dancing
Over a menu-card, scorn and adore
Prostitutes and skinny flirts
Who crossing arms and tossing skirts
High-kick – a quick
Eye captures all before they fall –
Quick lines, thick lines
Trace the huge ache under rouge.

'Cognac – more cognac!' Only the slop
Of a charwoman pushing her bucket and mop,
And the rattle of chairs on a table top.
The glass can fall no further. Time to stop
The charcoal's passionate waltzing with the hand.
Time to take up the hat, drag out the sticks,
And very slowly, like a hurt crab, stand:
With one wry bow to the vanished band,
Launch out with short steps harder than high kicks
Along the unspeakable inches of the street.
His flesh was his misfortune: but the feet
Of those whose flesh was all their fortune beat
Softly as the grey rain falling
Through his brain recalling
Marie, Annette, Jean-Claude and Marguerite.

Toulouse Lautrec
At the Moulin Rouge
The Art Institute of Chicago, Chicago

DELMORE SCHWARTZ

from

Seurat's Sunday Afternoon along the Seine

To Meyer and Lillian Schapiro

What are they looking at? Is it the river?
The sunlight on the river, the summer, leisure,
Or the luxury and nothingness of consciousness?
A little girl skips, a ring-tailed monkey hops
Like a kangaroo, held by a lady's lead
(Does the husband tax the Congo for the monkey's keep?)
The hopping monkey cannot follow the poodle dashing ahead.

Everyone holds his heart within his hands:

A prayer, a pledge of grace or gratitude
A devout offering to the god of summer, Sunday and plenitude.

The Sunday people are looking at hope itself.

They are looking at hope itself, under the sun, free from the teething
    anxiety, the gnawing nervousness
Which wastes so many days and years of consciousness.

The one who beholds them, beholding the gold and green
Of summer's Sunday is himself unseen. This is because he is
Dedicated radiance, supreme concentration, fanatically threading
The beads, needles and eyes – at once! – of vividness and permanence.
He is a saint of Sunday in the open air, a fanatic disciplined
By passion, courage, passion, skill, compassion, love: the love of life
    and the love of light as one, under the sun, with the love of life.

Everywhere radiance glows like a garden in stillness blossoming.

Many are looking, many are holding something or someone
Little or big: some hold several kinds of parasols:
Each one who holds an umbrella holds it differently

One hunches under his red umbrella as if he hid
And looked forth at the river secretly, or sought to be
Free of all of the others' judgement and proximity.
Next to him sits a lady who has turned to stone, or become a boulder,
Although her bell-and-sash hat is red.
A little girl holds to her mother's arm
As if it were a permanent genuine certainty:
Her broad-brimmed hat is blue and white, blue like the river, like the
    sailboats white,

Georges Seurat
Sunday Afternoon on the 'Ile de la Grande Jatte'
The Art Institute of Chicago, Chicago

And her face and her look have all the bland innocence,
Open and far from fear as cherubims playing harpsichords.
An adolescent girl holds a bouquet of flowers
As if she gazed and sought her unknown, hoped-for, dreaded destiny.
No hold is as strong as the strength with which the trees,
Grip the ground, curve up to the light, abide in the warm kind air:
Rooted and rising with a perfected tenacity
Beyond the distracted erratic case of mankind there.
Every umbrella curves and becomes a tree,
And the trees curving, arise to become and be
Like the umbrella, the bells of Sunday, summer, and Sunday's luxury.
Assured as the trees is the strolling dignity
Of the bourgeois wife who holds her husband's arm
With the easy confidence and pride of one who is
– She is sure – a sovereign Victorian empress and queen.
Her husband's dignity is as solid as his *embonpoint*:
He holds a good cigar, and a dainty cane, quite carelessly.
He is held by his wife, they are each other's property,
Dressed quietly and impeccably, they are suave and grave
As if they were unaware or free of time, and the grave,
Master and mistress of Sunday's promenade – of everything!
– As they are absolute monarchs of the ring-tailed monkey.
If you look long enough at anything
It will become extremely interesting;
If you look very long at anything
It will become rich, manifold, fascinating:

If you can look at any thing for long enough,
You will rejoice in the miracle of love,

You will possess and be blessed by the marvellous blinding radiance
  of love, you will be radiance.
Selfhood will possess and be possessed, as in the consecration of
  marriage, the mastery of vocation, the mystery of gift's mastery, the
  deathless relation of parenthood and progeny.
All things are fixed in one direction:
  We move with the Sunday people from right to left.

PART III

MODERN VOICES, MODERN VISIONS

LAWRENCE FERLINGHETTI

Short Story on a Painting of Gustav Klimt

They are kneeling upright on a flowered bed
He
    has just caught her there
             and holds her still
  Her gown
      has slipped down
           off her shoulder
  He has an urgent hunger
      His dark head
         bends to hers
          hungrily
And the woman the woman
  turns her tangerine lips from his
      one hand like the head of a dead swan
     draped down over
          his heavy neck
     the fingers
       strangely crimped
         tightly together
  her other arm doubled up
       against her tight breast
  her hand a languid claw
        clutching his hand
    which would turn her mouth
          to his
  her long dress made
      of multicolored blossoms
     quilted on gold
  her Titian hair
    with blue stars in it

Gustav Klimt
The Kiss
Osterreichische Galerie, Vienna

And his gold
                harlequin robe
                        checkered with
                                dark squares
        Gold garlands
                stream down over
                        her bare calves &
                                tensed feet
Nearby there must be
                a jeweled tree
                        with glass leaves aglitter
                                in the gold air
        It must be
                morning
                        in a faraway place somewhere
They
        are silent together
                        as in a flowered field
                upon the summer couch
                        which must be hers
        And he holds her still
                        so passionately
                holds her head to his
                        so gently so insistently
                to make her turn
                        her lips to his
        her eyes are closed
                        like folded petals
        She
                will not open
                        He
                        is not the One

Blue

1
Blue arrived. And its time was painted.
2
How many blues did the Mediterranean give?
3
Venus, mother of the sea of the blues.
4
The blue of the Greeks
rests, like a god, on columns.
5
The delicate, medieval blue:
6
The Virgin brought her virginal blue:
blue Mary, blue Our Lady.
7
It fell to his palette, And brought
the most secret blue from the sky.
Kneeling, he painted his blues.
Angels christened him with blue.
They appointed him: Beato Blue Angelico.
8
There are celestial palettes like wings
descended from the white of clouds.
9
The blues of Italy,
the blues of Spain,
the blues of France . . .
10
Raphael had wings.
Perugino also had wings
in order to spread his blues around.

11
When they get color from you,
indigo blue, brushes are feathers.

12
Venice of golden Titian blue.

13
Rome of Poussin blues between the pines.

14
Tintoretto blues embitter me.

15
Sulphur alcohol phosphorous Greco blue.
Toxic verdigris blue Greco.

16
On the palette of Velasquez I have
another name: I am called Guadarrama.

17
When I wander through nacreous flesh,
I am called the merry blue vein of Rubens.

18
And in the dawn of the lakes,
with a blue awakening, the echoes
of darkness repeat: Patinir.

19
There is a virginal Murillo blue,
forerunner of the brilliance of the chromes

20
Tiepolo also gave blues to his century.

21
Thinned, delicate, I am a sash –
Goya's light blue ribbon.

22
I would say to you:
                        – You are beautiful,
beautiful as the glorious blue of ceilings.

23
Explosions of blue in the allegories.

24
In Manet blue echoes sing
of a far off Spanish blue.

25
I am also called Renoir. They yell for me,
but I respond at times in lilac
with my blue voice made transparent.

26
I am the blue shadow,
the clear silhouette of your body.
For old eyes, the scandal.

27
The Balearics gave their blues to Painting.

28
Sometimes the sea invades the palette
of the painter and assigns him
a blue sky given only in secret.

29
The shadow is bluest when the body
that casts it has vanished.

30
Ecstatic blue, having been
pure blue in motion, is nostalgic.

31
Even if the blue is not in the picture,
it covers it like a screen of light.

32
One day blue said:
– Today I have a new name. They call me:
Blue Pablo Ruiz Blue Picasso.

Translated by Mark Strand

WALLACE STEVENS

from

The Man with the Blue Guitar

I

The man bent over his guitar,
A shearsman of sorts. The day was green.

They said, 'You have a blue guitar,
You do not play things as they are.'

The man replied, 'Things as they are
Are changed upon the blue guitar.'

And they said then, 'But play, you must,
A tune beyond us, yet ourselves,

A tune upon the blue guitar
Of things exactly as they are.'

II

I cannot bring a world quite round,
Although I patch it as I can.

I sing a hero's head, large eye
And bearded bronze, but not a man,

Although I patch him as I can
And reach through him almost to man,

If to serenade almost to man
Is to miss, by that, things as they are,

Say that it is the serenade
Of a man that plays a blue guitar.

Pablo Picasso
The Old Guitarist
The Art Institute of Chicago, Chicago

TONY CURTIS

Spring Fed

the stone basin
fills and fills
from the swivel tap's
trickle.

The hills have shed
so much snow
and now,
the first brown grasses
clear of it,
the heifers push
up into the fields
to take the early shoots.

And it comes
again
the whole slow
turning of the season –
the softer touch of air,
the shine on the bucket,
the unclenching of things,
the lapping of the water
in the stone basin
up to the rim,
and the very first,
this
delicious overspilling
onto our boots.

Andrew Wyeth
Spring Fed
Private Collection

DEREK MAHON

Girls on the Bridge

Audible trout,
Notional midges. Beds,
Lamplight and crisp linen, wait
In the house there for the sedate
Limbs and averted heads
Of the girls out

Late on the bridge.
The dusty road that slopes
Past is perhaps the main road south,
A symbol of world-wondering youth,
Of adolescent hopes
And privileges;

But stops to find
The girls content to gaze
At the unplumbed, reflective lake,
Their plangent conversational quack
Expressive of calm days
And peace of mind.

Grave daughters
Of time, you lightly toss
Your hair as the long shadows grow
And night begins to fall. Although
Your laughter calls across
The dark waters,

A ghastly sun
Watches in pale dismay.
Oh, you may laugh, being as you are
Fair sisters of the evening star,
But wait – if not today
A day will dawn

Eduard Munch
Girls on the Bridge
Wallraf-Richartz-Museum, Cologne

When the bad dreams
You hardly know will scatter
The punctual increment of your lives.
The road resumes, and where it curves,
A mile from where you chatter,
Somebody screams . . .

IRVING FELDMAN

Who Is Dora? What Is She?

Perhaps on such a day as this – but
in France in 1936, before,
that is, the War and other events
now too infinite to list (though
out-of-doors the oak whispers not
and the birds exist much as
they did and will) came and went
like that and like this, all things
that time bore and then dismissed
– before the War perhaps, on such
a day as this, Dora Maar (let us
say 'Dora Maar,' for who would be
anonymous? and her name was all
she really wore) sat in a chair
in 19 and 36 with a wish fierce
and commonplace to be mysterious,
to survive and to thrive, to be a success
and be good, and be covered
with paint like a kiss,
eternally, in nineteen hundred and thirty-six.

from 'Portrait de Femme' *After Picasso*

Pablo Picasso
Dora Maar Seated
Tate Gallery, London

X. J. KENNEDY

Nude Descending a Staircase

Toe upon toe, a snowing flesh,
A gold of lemon, root and rind,
She sifts in sunlight down the stairs
With nothing on. Nor on her mind.

We spy beneath the banister
A constant thresh of thigh on thigh –
Her lips imprint the swinging air
That parts to let her parts go by.

One-woman waterfall, she wears
Her slow descent like a long cape
And pausing, on the final stair
Collects her motions into shape.

Marcel Duchamp
Nude Descending a Staircase
Philadelphia Museum of Art, Philadelphia

CAROL ANN DUFFY

Standing Female Nude

Six hours like this for a few francs.
Belly nipple arse in the window light,
he drains the colour from me. Further to the right,
Madame. And do try to be still.
I shall be represented analytically and hung
in great museums. The bourgeoisie will coo
at such an image of a river-whore. They call it Art.

Maybe. He is concerned with volume, space.
I with the next meal. You're getting thin,
Madame, this is not good. My breasts hang
slightly low, the studio is cold. In the tealeaves
I can see the Queen of England gazing
on my shape. Magnificent, she murmurs
moving on. It makes me laugh. His name

is Georges. He tells me he's a genius.
There are times he does not concentrate
and stiffens for my warmth. Men think of their mothers.
He possesses me on canvas as he dips the brush
repeatedly into the paint. Little man,
you've not the money for the arts I sell.
Both poor, we make our living how we can.

I ask him Why do you do this? Because
I have to. There's no choice. Don't talk.
My smile confuses him. These artists
take themselves too seriously. At night I fill myself
with wine and dance around the bars. When it's finished
he shows me proudly, lights a cigarette. I say
twelve francs and get my shawl. It does not look like me.

Georges Braque
Bather
Tate Gallery, London

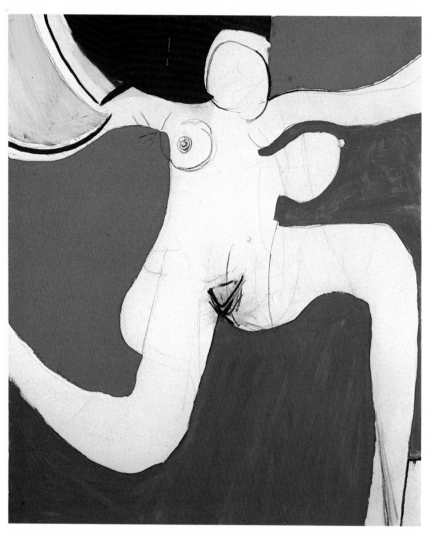

Roger Hilton
Oi yoi yoi
Tate Gallery, London

VICKI FEAVER

Oi yoi yoi

(to Roger Hilton about his painting in the Tate)

The lady has no shame.
Wearing not a stitch
she is lolloping across
an abstract beach
towards a notional sea.

I like the whisker
of hair under her armpit.
It suggests that she's not
one of those women who's always
trying to get rid of their smell.

You were more interested
in her swinging baroque tits
and the space between her thighs
than the expression on her face.
That you've left blank.

But her mons venus
you've etched in black ink
with the exuberance of a young lad
caught short on a bellyful of beer
scrawling on the wall in the Gents.

As a woman I ought to object.
But she looks happy enough.
And which of us doesn't occasionally
want one of the Old Gods to come down
and chase us over the sands.

MICHAEL LONGLEY

Man Lying on a Wall

Homage to L.S. Lowry

You could draw a straight line from the heels,
Through calves, buttocks and shoulderblades
To the back of the head: pressure points
That bear the enormous weight of the sky.
Should you take away the supporting structure
The result would be a miracle or
An extremely clever conjuring trick.
As it is, the man lying on the wall
Is wearing the serious expression
Of popes and kings in their final slumber,
His deportment not dissimilar to
Their stiff, reluctant exits from this world
Above the shoulders of the multitude.

It is difficult to judge whether or not
He is sleeping or merely disinclined
To arrive punctually at the office
Or to return home in time for his tea.
He is wearing a pinstripe suit, black shoes
And a bowler hat: on the pavement
Below him, like a relic or something
He is trying to forget, his briefcase
With everybody's initials on it.

L.S. Lowry
Man Lying on a Wall
City Art Gallery & Museum, Salford

MICHAEL HAMBURGER

A Painter Painted

Portrait or nature morte or landscape (nature vivante) –
Pencil and brush make all a still life, fixed,
So that the wind that swept, breath that came hard
Or easy, when wind has dropped, breath has passed on,
The never visible, may stir again in stillness.

Visible both, the painter and the painted
Passed by me, four decades ago. We met,
We talked, we drank, and we went our ways.
This head's more true than the head I saw.
Closed, these lips tell me more than the lips that spoke.
Lowered, these eyes are better at looking.

A likeness caught? No. Pictor invenit.
Slowly, slowly, under his lowered eyelids
He worked, against time, to find the face grown truer,
Coax it to life in paint's dead millimetres,
Compose them into nature, in a light
That is not London's, any hour's or year's;

Furrow it, too, with darkness; let in the winds
That left their roads, painter's and painted's, littered,
Brought branches down, scattering feathers, fruit,
Though for a moment only, stopped the bland flow of breath.

And here it hangs, the still life of a head.

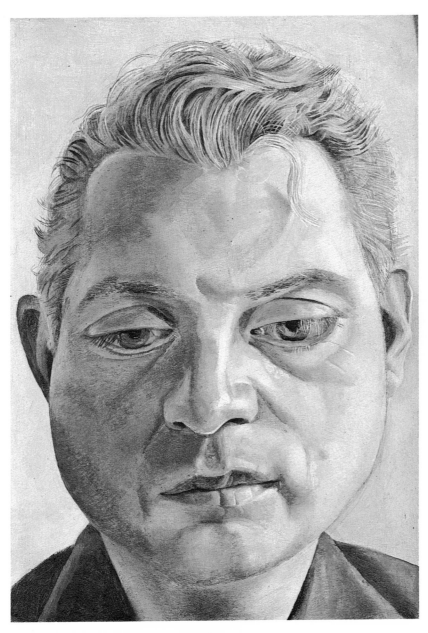

Lucian Freud
Francis Bacon
Tate Gallery, London

THOMAS BLACKBURN

Francis Bacon

The crumpled sheets of the bed of murder
You showed me how the creases, stains and folds
Make the crime perpetually occur,
The resonance and the mystery of details.

I remember the chaos of cuttings and paint,
The colours on the plate in your studio,
How you called Jesus a queen but very quaint
I disagreed but agreed with your cult of horror

And collected pictures in an old scrap book,
A dying drunk, boxers, an addict of heroin,
Many variants on the theme of pain and shock;
I shudder at them now, they were pleasant then.

Degradation, not degraded yourself, your fascination
All the varieties of misery and mania;
You called it closing in to the nerve; I leant upon
The enormity of the creature that you are

And made poems underneath your cast shadow,
Exploring the terror of bearing humanity
And relishing – what it was I still don't know,
Something about breaking out of contour into mystery.

Now at sixty one and having learnt compassion,
Some insight from confusion and despair
I seek the pities, how to make confusion
Both in myself and others breathe fresher air.

And marvel at you, very rich and famous,
Still crucified by what takes place in a bed,
And uttering, with superb technique, pretentious
Platitudes of rut, that you have said and said.

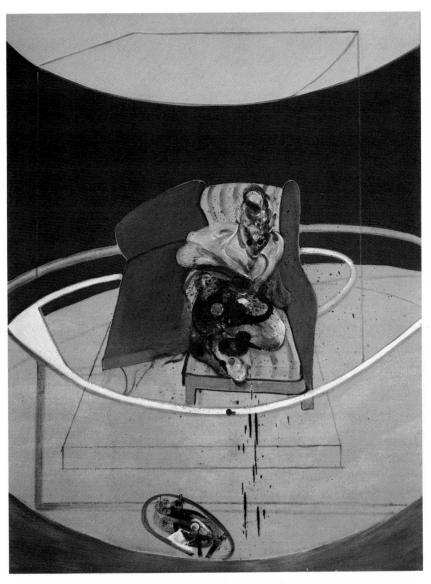

Francis Bacon
Study for Portrait on Folding Bed
Tate Gallery, London

Totes Meer – by Paul Nash, 1940–41

1

This picture is of waste. No victory
gloats in the absent eye that we make ours
by seeing what it saw. But tragedy
is not stressed either – we may keep our tears.

No beggar whimpers for them, we are shown
no scars, no mutilations, no burnt boys
but, bleached by moonlight, aircraft wreckage thrown
into an open grave for broken toys.

An Icarus has fallen from the sky.
Another and another fall, a rain
of torches must have fallen. This clear eye
records the waste, does not insist on pain.

Pity withheld is power; a reservoir
of weeping gathers, war-dammed in the brain.

2

The time is dawn. The moon
hangs on withdrawing dark
shedding just light enough
to cast shadows that mark
the sand. On ragged waves –
as rigid in arrest
as signpost dead – each crest
postures as though it lives,
threatens but cannot reach
with more than shadow-claws
the dead sea's desert beach:
yet this dry tide still gnaws
the fields away; lost land
submerges, all but drowned.

Paul Nash
Totes Meer (Dead Sea)
Tate Gallery, London

[133]

GILLIAN CLARKE

The Rothko Room

He crushed charcoal with a city's rubies
saw such visions of soft-edged night and day
as stop the ears with silence. In this,
the last room after hours in the gallery,
a mesh diffuses London's light and sound.
The Indian keeper nods to sleep, marooned
in a trapezium of black on red.

We few who stop are quiet as if we prayed
in this room after Turner's turbulence.
Coming and going through paint's water-curtains
turning a corner suddenly we find
a city burns, a cathedral comes down
with a last blaze filling its gaudy lantern
and windows buckle as a tenement falls.

Rack the heart for memory or sense
and reds like these come crowding out of dream:
musk mallow, goat's rue, impatiens,
loosestrife, hellebore, belladonna, nightshade,
poppysilks crushed in their velvety soot,
and digitalis purpurea, red on maroon,
drop dappled gloves along an August lane.

A morning's laundry marking glass with steam
on rainy Mondays where a blackbird sings
sodden in dripping dark-red lilac trees.
We look, myopic, down his corridors
through misted spectacles of broken glass
window on window, scaffolding of pain
red on maroon and black, black on maroon.

Mark Rothko
Red on Maroon
Tate Gallery, London

JOHN FULLER

The Money of their Colour;
or, The American Express-ionists

When you just can't afford a de Kooning
Since you're certain you haven't the cash
And the prices are simply ballooning
And your accountant condemns it as rash,
No need to resort to impugning
Their worth, like a Philistine.
'How will you pay?' asks de Kooning.
'That'll do nicely,' says Kline.

You see, they will give you some credit
For a trusting belief in their stuff.
A masterpiece? Sweetie, you've said it!
And a plain master *card* is enough.
You stand there quietly swooning
At a crushed Private View, over wine:
'How will you pay?' asks de Kooning.
'That'll do nicely,' says Kline.

The 'integrity of the surface'
Means the figure they ask is elastic,
But if dollars are making you nervous
Just hand over a small piece of plastic
To the painter, who sits there crooning
A chorus of *Auld Lang Syne*.
'How will you pay?' asks de Kooning.
'That'll do nicely,' says Kline.

The effort you need's superhuman
Finding Rothkos (at best) second-hand.
The teeniest Barnett Newman
Will cost you a hundred grand.
But don't just sit about mooning:
Put your name on the dotted line!
'How will you pay?' asks de Kooning.
'That'll do nicely,' says Kline.

If money is merely a figment
Of Pollock's imagination
Then how does he pay for the pigment
That he leaks in the rage of creation?
After years of financial fine-tuning
He knows an account is divine:
'How will you pay?' asks de Kooning.
'Have a nice day,' says Kline.

JOHN CASSIDY

Reflections on the purchase by a Municipal Gallery of Three Heads by Henry Moore

'Look at what it costs them, too.
It makes you wonder what we pay rates
For.
Difficulty finding a site, they said
They had. It was in the paper.
Twice.
I mean look at them, they're not human.
No one can say there's any beauty
There.
You saw that letter to the editor?
I think that fairly put them in their place:
Sir,
As a humble citizen who foots the bill,
If I might be permitted to suggest
A site,
The bottom of the Old Mill Lodge would seem
To me a suitable venue. Yours
Truly.
Neat, wasn't it? I mean it shows
What people think. I've never held with these
Experts.'

They stand instead where light comes through the
    ceiling,
Watery within the greenish walls.
They watch,
Sockets of smooth metal and spiky metal,
Small, unhuman, hollow, but definitely
Heads.
Too quizzical they are. They ask you questions.
Look at them and they'll remind you of
Things.
Three of them standing there. Outlaws. They're not
Properly in accord with what people
Think.

W.B. YEATS

The Municipal Gallery Revisited

I

Around me the images of thirty years:
An ambush; pilgrims at the water-side;
Casement upon trial, half hidden by the bars,
Guarded; Griffith staring in hysterical pride;
Kevin O'Higgins' countenance that wears
A gentle questioning look that cannot hide
A soul incapable of remorse or rest;
A revolutionary soldier kneeling to be blessed;

II

An Abbot or Archbishop with an upraised hand
Blessing the Tricolour. 'This is not,' I say,
'The dead Ireland of my youth, but an Ireland
The poets have imagined, terrible and gay.'
Before a woman's portrait suddenly I stand,
Beautiful and gentle in her Venetian way.
I met her all but fifty years ago
For twenty minutes in some studio.

III

Heart-smitten with emotion I sink down,
My heart recovering with covered eyes;
Wherever I had looked I had looked upon
My permanent or impermanent images:
Augusta Gregory's son; her sister's son,
Hugh Lane, 'onlie begetter' of all these;
Hazel Lavery living and dying, that tale
As though some ballad-singer had sung it all;

Antonio Mancini
Lady Gregory
The Hugh Lane Municipal Gallery of Modern Art, Dublin

IV

Mancini's portrait of Augusta Gregory,
'Greatest since Rembrandt,' according to John Synge;
A great ebullient portrait certainly;
But where is the brush that could show anything
Of all that pride and that humility?
And I am in despair that time may bring
Approved patterns of women or of men
But not that selfsame excellence again.

V

My mediaeval knees lack health until they bend,
But in that woman, in that household where
Honour had lived so long, all lacking found.
Childless I thought, 'My children may find here
Deep-rooted things,' but never foresaw its end,
And now that end has come I have not wept;
No fox can foul the lair the badger swept –

VI

(An image out of Spenser and the common tongue).
John Synge, I and Augusta Gregory, thought
All that we did, all that we said or sang
Must come from contact with the soil, from that
Contact everything Antaeus-like grew strong.
We three alone in modern times had brought
Everything down to that sole test again,
Dream of the noble and the beggar-man.

VII

And here's John Synge himself, that rooted man,
'Forgetting human words,' a grave deep face.
You that would judge me, do not judge alone
This book or that, come to this hallowed place
Where my friends' portraits hang and look thereon;
Ireland's history in their lineaments trace;
Think where man's glory most begins and ends,
And say my glory was I had such friends.

ROBERT WALLACE

Giacometti's Dog

lopes in bronze:
    scruffy,
        thin. In

the Museum of Modern Art
    head
        down, neck long as sadness

lowering to hanging ears
    (he's eyeless)
        that hear

nothing, and the sausage
    muzzle
        that leads him as

surely as eyes:
    he might
        be

dead, dried webs or clots of flesh
    and fur
        on the thin, long bones – but

isn't, obviously,
    is obviously
        traveling intent on his

own aim: legs
    lofting
        with a gaiety the dead aren't known

for. Going
    onward in one place,
        he doesn't so much ignore

Alberto Giacometti
The Dog
*Foundation Alberto Giacometti,
Kunsthaus, Zürich*

[143]

as not recognize
        the well-
                dressed Sunday hun-

dreds who passing, pausing make
        his bronze
                road

move. Why
        do they come to admire
                him,

who wouldn't care for real dogs
        less raggy
                than he

is? It's his tragic
        insouciance
                bugs them? or is

it that art can make us
        cherish
                anything – this command

of shaping and abutting space –
        that makes us love
                even mutts,

even the world, having
        rocks
                and the wind for comrades?

It's not this starved hound,
        but Giacometti seeing
                him we see.

We'll stand in line all day
        to see one man
                love anything enough.

W.S. GRAHAM

The Thermal Stair

(In memory of Peter Lanyon)

I called today, Peter, and you were away.
I look out over Botallack and over Ding
Dong and Levant and over the jasper sea.

Find me a thermal to speak and soar to you from
Over Lanyon Quoit and the circling stones standing
High on the moor over Gurnard's Head where some

Time three foxglove summers ago, you came.
The days are shortening over Little Parc Owles.
The poet or painter steers his life to maim

Himself somehow for the job. His job is Love
Imagined into words or paint to make
An object that will stand and will not move.

Peter, I called and you were away, speaking
Only through what you made and at your best.
Look, there above Botallack, the buzzard riding

The salt updraught slides off the broken air
And out of sight to quarter a new place.
The Celtic sea, the Methodist sea is there.

You said once in the Engine
House below Morvah
That words make their world
In the same way as the painter's
Mark surprises him
Into seeing new.

Sit here on the sparstone
In this ruin where
Once the early beam
Engine pounded and broke
The air with industry.

Now the chuck of daws
And the listening sea.

'Shall we go down' you said
'Before the light goes
And stand below the old
Tin-workings around
Morvah and St Just?'
You said 'Here is the sea
Made by alfred wallis
Or any poet's or painter's
Eye it encounters.
Or is it better made
By all those vesselled men
Sometime it maintained?
We all make it again.'

Give me your hand, Peter,
To steady me on the word.

Seventy-two by sixty,
Italy hangs on the wall.
A woman stands with a drink
In some polite place
And looks at SARACINESCO
And turns to mention space.
That one if she could
Would ride Artistically
The thermals you once rode.

Peter Lanyon
Thermal
Tate Gallery, London

Peter, the phallic boys
Begin to wink their lights.
Godrevy and the Wolf
Are calling Opening Time.
We'll take the quickest way
The tin singers made.
Climb here where the hand
Will not grasp on air.
And that dark-suited man
Has set the dominoes out
On the Queen's table.
Peter, we'll sit and drink
And go in the sea's roar
To Labrador with Wallis
Or rise on Lanyon's stair:

Uneasy, lovable man, give me your painting
Hand to steady me taking the word-road home.
Lanyon, why is it you're earlier away?
Remember me wherever you listen from.
Lanyon, dingdong dingdong from carn to carn.
It seems tonight all Closing bells are tolling
Across the Duchy shire wherever I turn.

ANTHONY CRONIN

Lines For a Painter

to Patrick Swift

The tree grew under your hand one day,
So many shades of green growing over the white
Canvas, as through the actual leaves outside the window
And through the open window onto the canvas fell the
     light.

And I sat on the bed trying unsuccessfully to write,
Envying you the union of the painter's mind and hand,
The contact of brush with canvas, the physical communion,
The external identity of the object and the painting you
     had planned;

For among the shards of memory nothing that day would
     grow
Of its own accord,
And I thought I could never see, as you saw the tree on
     the canvas,
One draughtsman's word.

Only inside the mind,
In the rubble of thought,
Were the pro-and-con, prose-growing, all too argumentative
Poems I sought.

Whereas there in Camden Town
In the petrol fumes and gold of a London summer was the
     tree you drew,
As you might find anywhere, inside or outside the studio,
     something
Which was itself, not you.

Patrick Swift
Tree in Camden Town
Private Collection

Well envying I have said,
But that evening as we walked
Through the cooling twilight down
To the pub and talked

I saw what in truth I had envied –
Not in fact
That you were released from any obligation,
Or that the act

Of painting was less or more objective
Than thinking the word –
But that, like poems, your painting
Was of course the reward

Of the true self yielding to appearances
Outside its power
While still in the dominion of love asseverating
Its absolute hour.

W.R. Sickert
The Blackbird of Paradise
City Art Gallery, Leeds

W.H. DAVIES

The Bird of Paradise

Here comes Kate Summers who, for gold,
   Takes any man to bed:
'You knew my friend, Nell Barnes,' said she;
   'You knew Nell Barnes – she's dead.

'Nell Barnes was bad on all you men,
   Unclean, a thief as well;
Yet all my life I have not found
   A better friend than Nell.

'So I sat at her side at last,
   For hours till she was dead;
And yet she had no sense at all
   Of any word I said.

'For all her cry but came to this –
   "Not for the world! Take care:
Don't touch that bird of paradise,
   Perched on the bedpost there!"

'I asked her would she like some grapes,
   Some damsons ripe and sweet;
A custard made with new-laid eggs,
   Or tender fowl to eat.

'I promised I would follow her,
   To see her in her grave;
And buy a wreath with borrowed pence,
   If nothing I could save.

'Yet still her cry but came to this –
   "Not for the world! Take care:
Don't touch that bird of paradise,
   Perched on the bedpost there!"'

Do not go gentle into that good night

Do not go gentle into that good night,
Old age should burn and rave at close of day;
Rage, rage against the dying of the light.

Though wise men at their end know dark is right,
Because their words had forked no lightning they
Do not go gentle into that good night.

Good men, the last wave by, crying how bright
Their frail deeds might have danced in a green bay,
Rage, rage against the dying of the light.

Wild men who caught and sang the sun in flight,
And learn, too late, they grieved it on its way,
Do not go gentle into that good night.

Grave men, near death, who see with blinding sight
Blind eyes could blaze like meteors and be gay,
Rage, rage against the dying of the light.

And you, my father, there on the sad height,
Curse, bless, me now with your fierce tears, I pray.
Do no go gentle into that good night.
Rage, rage against the dying of the light.

Ceri Richards
Do not go gentle into that good night
Tate Gallery, London

PART IV
—

CORRESPONDENCES

T.S. ELIOT

Lines for Cuscuscaraway and
Mirza Murad Ali Beg

How unpleasant to meet Mr. Eliot!
With his features of clerical cut,
And his brow so grim
And his mouth so prim
And his conversation, so nicely
Restricted to What Precisely
And If and Perhaps and But.
How unpleasant to meet Mr. Eliot!
With a bobtail cur
In a coat of fur
And a porpentine cat
And a wopsical hat:
How unpleasant to meet Mr. Eliot!
        (Whether his mouth be open or shut)

Patrick Heron
T.S. Eliot
National Portrait Gallery, London

The Face in the Mirror

Grey haunted eyes, absent-mindedly glaring
From wide, uneven orbits; one brow drooping
Somewhat over the eye
Because of a missile fragment still inhering,
Skin deep, as a foolish record of old-world fighting.

Crookedly broken nose – low tackling caused it;
Cheeks, furrowed; coarse grey hair, flying frenetic;
Forehead, wrinkled and high;
Jowls, prominent; ears, large; jaw, pugilistic;
Teeth, few; lips, full and ruddy; mouth, ascetic.

I pause with razor poised, scowling derision
At the mirrored man whose beard needs my attention
And once more ask him why
He still stands ready, with a boy's presumption,
To court the queen in her high silk pavilion.

John Aldridge
Robert Graves
National Portrait Gallery, London

CHARLES TOMLINSON

Paring the Apple

There are portraits and still-lifes.

And there is paring the apple.

And then? Paring it slowly,
From under cool-yellow
Cold-white emerging. And . . . ?

The spring of concentric peel
Unwinding off white,
The blade hidden, dividing.

There are portraits and still-lifes
And the first, because 'human'
Does not excel the second, and
Neither is less weighted
With a human gesture, than paring the apple
With a human stillness.

The cool blade
Severs between coolness, apple-rind
Compelling a recognition.

Pieter de Hoogh
Woman Peeling Apples
Wallace Collection, London

TED HUGHES

To Paint a Water Lily

A green level of lily leaves
Roofs the pond's chamber and paves

The flies' furious arena: study
These, the two minds of this lady.

First observe the air's dragonfly
That eats meat, that bullets by

Or stands in space to take aim;
Others as dangerous comb the hum

Under the trees. There are battle-shouts
And death-cries everywhere hereabouts

But inaudible, so the eyes praise
To see the colours of these flies

Rainbow their arcs, spark, or settle
Cooling like beads of molten metal

Through the spectrum. Think what worse
Is the pond-bed's matter of course;

Prehistoric bedragonned times
Crawl that darkness with Latin names,

Have evolved no improvements there,
Jaws for heads, the set stare,

Ignorant of age as of hour –
Now paint the long-necked lily-flower

Which, deep in both worlds, can be still
As a painting, trembling hardly at all

Though the dragonfly alight,
Whatever horror nudge her root.

Claude Monet
La Bassin aux Nymphéas
National Gallery, London

JACQUES PRÉVERT

How to Paint the Portrait of a Bird

First paint a cage
with an open door
then paint
something pretty
something simple
something fine
something useful
for the bird
next place the canvas against a tree
in a garden
in a wood
or in a forest
hide behind the tree
without speaking
without moving. . . .
Sometimes the bird comes quickly
but it can take many years
before making up its mind
Don't be discouraged
wait
wait if necessary for years
the quickness or the slowness of the coming
of the bird having no relation
to the success of the picture
When the bird comes
if it comes
observe the deepest silence
wait for the bird to enter the cage
and when it has entered
gently close the door with the paint-brush
then
one by one paint-out all the bars
taking care not to touch one feather of the bird
Next make a portrait of the tree
choosing the finest of its branches
for the bird

Georges Braque
School Prints – 'The Bird'
Tate Gallery, London

paint also the green leaves and the freshness of the wind
dust in the sun
and the sound of the grazing cattle in the heat of summer
and wait for the bird to decide to sing
If the bird does not sing
it is a bad sign
a sign that the picture is bad
but if it sings it is a good sign
a sign that you are ready to sign
so then you pluck very gently
one of the quills of the bird
and you write your name in a corner of the picture.

Translated by Paul Dehn

JOHN COTTON

Old Movies

How I loved those old movies
they would show in the Roxys
and Regals amongst all that
gilt plaster, or in the Bijou
flea-pits smelling of Jeyes.
The men sleek haired and suited,
with white cuffs and big trilbies,
their girls all pushovers,
wide-eyed with lashes
like venus fly traps and their
clouds of blonde candyfloss
for hair. Oh those bosoms, hips
and those long long legs
I never saw in daylight!
And their apartments,
vast as temples,
full of unused furniture,
the sideboards bending with booze,
and all those acres of bed!
She, in attendance, wearing
diaphanous, but never quite
diaphanous enough, nightwear.
And their lives!
Where the baddies only,
if not always, stopped one,
and they loved and loved
and never ended up married.
Every time I get a whiff
of that disinfectant
I feel nostalgic.

William Roberts
The Cinema
Tate Gallery, London

LOUIS MACNEICE

from

Circus

I

Trapezists

Intricacy of engines,
Delicacy of darkness;
They rise into the tent's
Top like deep-sea divers

And hooked from the mouth like fish
Frame their frolic
Above the silent music
And the awed audience,

Hang by their teeth
Beneath the cone of canvas,
The ring beneath them
An eye that is empty

Who live in a world
Of aery technic
Like dolls or angels
Sexless and simple

Our fear their frame,
Hallowed by handclaps,
Honoured by eyes
Upward in incense.

On the tent's walls
Fourfold shadowed
In a crucifixion's
Endless moment

Intricacy of,
Delicacy of,
Darkness and engines.

Marc Chagall
Blue Circus
Tate Gallery, London

[171]

II
Horses

The long whip lingers,
Toys with the sawdust;
The horses amble
On a disc of dreams.

The drumsticks flower
In pink percussion
To mix with the metal
Petals of brass.

The needle runs
In narrower circles;
The long whip leaps
And leads them inward.

Piebald horses
And ribald music
Circle around
A spangled lady.

III
Clowns
Clowns, Clowns and
Clowns
A firm that furthers
Nobody's business

Zanies by royal
Charter and adept
At false addition
And gay combustion

With bladders for batons
And upright eyebrows
Flappers for feet
And figs for no one.

The child's face pops
Like ginger beer
To see the air
Alive with bowlers.

Bric-a-brac
Pick-a-back
Spillbucket
Splits.

VERNON SCANNELL

They Did Not Expect This

They did not expect this. Being neither wise nor brave
And wearing only the beauty of youth's season
They took the first turning quite unquestioningly
And walked quickly without looking back even once.

It was of course the wrong turning. First they were nagged
By a small wind that tugged at their clothing like a dog;
Then the rain began and there was no shelter anywhere,
Only the street and the rows of houses stern as soldiers.

Though the blood chilled, the endearing word burnt the tongue.
There were no parks or gardens or public houses:
Midnight settled and the rain paused leaving the city
Enormous and still like a great sleeping seal.

At last they found accommodation in a cold
Furnished room where they quickly learnt to believe in ghosts;
They had their hope stuffed and put on the mantelpiece
But found, after a while, that they did not notice it.

While she spends many hours looking in the bottoms of teacups
He reads much about association football
And waits for the marvellous envelope to fall:
Their eyes are strangers and they rarely speak.
                                    They did not expect this.

Walter Sickert
Ennui
Tate Gallery, London

ANTHONY THWAITE

The Bonfire

Day by day, day after day, we fed it
With straw, mown grass, shavings, shaken weeds,
The huge flat leaves of umbrella plants, old spoil
Left by the builders, combustible; yet it
Coughed fitfully at the touch of a match,
Flared briefly, spat flame through a few dry seeds
Like a chain of fireworks, then slumped back to the soil
Smouldering and smoky, leaving us to watch

Only a heavy grey mantle without fire.
This glum construction seemed choked at heart,
The coils of newspaper burrowed into its hulk
Led our small flames into the middle of nowhere,
Never touching its centre, sodden with rot.
Ritual petrol sprinklings wouldn't make it start
But swerved and vanished over its squat brown bulk,
Still heavily sullen, grimly determined not

To do away with itself. A whiff of smoke
Hung over it as over a volcano.
Until one night, late, when we heard outside
A crackling roar, and saw the far field look
Like a Gehenna claiming its due dead.
The beacon beckoned, fierily aglow
With days of waiting, hiding deep inside
Its bided time, ravenous to be fed.

Sir John Millais
Autumn Leaves
Manchester City Art Galleries

Brother Fire

When our brother Fire was having his dog's day
Jumping the London streets with millions of tin cans
Clanking at his tail, we heard some shadow say
'Give the dog a bone' – and so we gave him ours;
Night after night we watched him slaver and crunch away
The beams of human life, the tops of topless towers.

Which gluttony of his for us was Lenten fare
Who mother-naked, suckled with sparks, were chill
Though cotted in a grill of sizzling air
Striped like a convict – black, yellow and red;
Thus were we weaned to knowledge of the Will
That wills the natural world but wills us dead.

O delicate walker, babbler, dialectician Fire,
O enemy and image of ourselves,
Did we not on those mornings after the All Clear,
When you were looting shops in elemental joy
And singing as you swarmed up city block and spire,
Echo your thought in ours? 'Destroy! Destroy!'

Henry Carr
St Clement Dane on Fire After Bombing
Imperial War Museum, London

Carel Weight
The Day of Doom
Private Collection

Fire

Fire, like all servants, must be watched
continually. Fire, the best servant,
therefore the most dangerous. Every
servant dreams to usurp his master, outdo
his arrogance and pomp, his whims, his cruelty.
Servants would create a world
of absolute caprice, a universe moved
by the same murderous totalitarian
ferocity as fire rioting through
tenements, incandescing block after block
of their pattern: a chart lit up to demonstrate
the saturation bombing (those who plot it
being fire's unwitting servants).
Once got loose, fire will eat metal box-cars
and girders, cement structures, papery bark
of eucalyptus trees, household pets or
humans: consume anything. Because nothing
is alien to fire, as the perfect servant
never shows surprise at his ruler's demands
but will supply whatever asked for. Contained,
fire can work miracles, but rampaging
free, reduces even his own hearth
to ashy desolation – then creeps back,
surly, to sit weeping in the ruins.

John Singer Sargent
Gassed
Imperial War Museum, London
(detail)

DOUGLAS DUNN

War Blinded

For more than sixty years he has been blind
Behind that wall, these trees, with terrible
Longevity wheeled in the sun and wind
On pathways of the soldiers' hospital.

For half that time his story's troubled me –
That showroom by the ferry, where I saw
His basketwork, a touch-turned filigree
His fingers coaxed from charitable straw;

Or how he felt when young, enlisting at
Recruiting tables on the football pitch,
To end up slumped across a parapet,
His eye-blood running in a molten ditch;

Or how the light looked when I saw two men,
One blind, one in a wheelchair, in that park,
Their dignity, which I have not forgotten,
Which helps me struggle with this lesser dark.

That war's too old for me to understand
How he might think, nursed now in wards of want,
Remembering that day when his right hand
Gripped on the shoulder of the man in front.

R.M. RILKE

The Raising of Lazarus

One had to bear with the majority –
what they wanted was a sign that screamed:
Martha, though, and Mary – he had dreamed
they would be contented just to see
that he *could*. But not a soul believed him:
'Lord, you've come too late,' said all the crowd.
So to peaceful Nature, though it grieved him,
on he went to do the unallowed.
Asked them, eyes half-shut, his body glowing
with anger, 'Where's the grave?' Tormentedly.
And to them it seemed his tears were flowing,
as they thronged behind him, curiously.
As he walked, the thing seemed monstrous to him,
childish, horrible experiment:
then there suddenly went flaming through him
such an all-consuming argument
against their life, their death, their whole collection
of separations made by them alone,
all his body quivered with rejection
as he gave out hoarsely 'Raise the stone'.
Someone shouted that the corpse was stinking
(buried now four days ago) – but He
stood erect, brim-full of that unblinking,
mounting gesture, that so painfully
lifted up his hand (no hand was ever
raised so slowly, so immeasurably),
till it stood there, shining in the gloom.
There it slowly, clawingly contracted:
what if all the dead should be attracted
upwards, through that syphon of a tomb,
where a pallid chrysalidal thing
was writhing up from where it had been lying? –
But it stood alone (no more replying),
and they saw a vague, unidentifying
Life compelled to give it harbouring.

Translated by J.B. Leishman

Vincent Van Gogh
Raising of Lazarus
National Museum Vincent Van Gogh,
Amsterdam

Leda and the Swan

A sudden blow: the great wings beating still
Above the staggering girl, her thighs caressed
By the dark webs, her nape caught in his bill,
He holds her helpless breast upon his breast.

How can those terrified vague fingers push
The feathered glory from her loosening thighs?
And how can body, laid in that white rush,
But feel the strange heart beating where it lies?

A shudder in the loins engenders there
The broken wall, the burning roof and tower
And Agamemnon dead.
                    Being so caught up,
So mastered by the brute blood of the air,
Did she put on his knowledge with his power
Before the indifferent beak could let her drop?

Marble relief
Leda and the Swan
British Museum, London

Helen

TEUCER: . . . *towards sea surrounded Cyprus, where Apollo said*
        I was to settle down and call my city's name
        Salamis, in memory of my old island home. . . .
HELEN: *I never went to Troy. Only a phantom went. . . .*
MESSENGER: *What's this? Then did we toil in vain there simply for a cloud?*
                         Euripedes, Helen

'The nightingales will never let you go to sleep at Platres.'

Shy nightingale, in the shuddering breath of the leaves,
Giver of dewy music, the dew of the forest,
To bodies parted each from each, to the souls
Of those who know that they will not come back again.
Blind voice, in the darkened memory turning over
Footsteps, gestures of hands, I'd not dare say kisses,
And the bitter heave of the heart, the heart of a slave grown savage.

'The nightingales will never let you go to sleep at Platres.'

Platres, what is it? Who is it knows this island?
I have lived my life hearing names heard for the first time;
New places and new madnesses
Whether of men or gods.
               My own fate which wavers
Between the final sword of an Ajax
And another Salamis
Has brought me to this shore; here the moon
Has risen from the sea like Aphrodite,
Has blotted out the Archer, and now she goes,
To the Heart of the Scorpion, changing everything.
O truth, where are you?
I also was an archer in the war;
My fate that of a man who missed the mark.

Melodious nightingale,
On such a night as this the Spartan slave girls
Heard you on Proteus's beach and lifted their lament.
And among them there was – who could have thought it? – Helen!
She, our pursuit for years beside Scamander.
She was there, at the desert's edge. I touched her. She spoke to me.
'It is not true, it is not true', she cried.
'I never went aboard that coloured ship;
I never trod the ground of manly Troy.'

Gustave Moreau
Helen at the Scaean Gate
Gustave Moreau Museum, Paris

Deep-girdled, the sun in her hair, with that way of standing,
The print of shadows and the print of smiles
On shoulders, thighs and knees,
The lively skin, the eyes and the great eyelids,
She was there, on the banks of a Delta.
                                        And at Troy?
Nothing. At Troy a phantom.
So the gods willed it.
And Paris lay with a shadow as though it were solid flesh:
And we were slaughtered for Helen ten long years.

Great pain had fallen on Greece.
So many bodies thrown
To jaws of the sea, to jaws of the earth;
So many souls
Given up to the mill-stones to be crushed like corn.
And the muddy beds of the rivers sweated with blood
For a wavering linen garment, a thing of air,
For a butterfly's jerk, for a swan's down, for a Helen.
And my brother?
                    O nightingale, nightingale,
What is god? What is not god? What is in-between?

'The nightingales will never let you go to sleep at Platres!'

Tearful bird,
            at sea-kissed Cyprus,
Ordained for me to remind me of my country,
I moored alone and brought this fairy story,
If it is true that it is a fairy story,
If it is true that man will not set in motion once more
The old deceit of the gods;
                            if it is true
That after many years some other Teucer,
Some Ajax, maybe, or Priam or Hecuba,
Or someone quite unknown, nameless, yet one who saw
The corpses crown the banks of a Scamander,
Were not so fated as this – fated to hear
The steps of messengers, who come to tell him
That so much suffering, so much of life
Fell into the abyss
For the sake of an empty garment, for a Helen.

Translated by Rex Warner

PART V

BELLISSIMA!

EDWARD LUCIE-SMITH

from 'Seven Colours' for Michael Rothenstein

Red

Spurt of blood. Colour of massacre.
And in Russian, so they tell me,
the adjective that means 'beautiful'.
I remember the red of icons,
robes for a saint or for the Virgin,
with gold and ultramarine,
a trinity of splendour. Red,
and again red. When I look too long,
I feel my pulse beating, there in the
vein that feeds the eyeball. The colour changed
to a musical throbbing. What do
suicides feel, as they see the blood
flow from the slit wrist, and spread in the
bathwater? Those rosy veils, wrapping
the discarded body. Precious
to the end, to the end ceremonious.

Yellow

I remember the white cat. Yellow
eyes at night in our garden, stalking
a bird on a branch. Those two golden
lanterns. When he looked at you, it was
like finding two suns in a snowball.
Yellow, too, the traces of urine
on snow, at the place where the drunk pissed
coming home through the winter city.

Proofs that the colour is changeable
in itself, and also in meaning.
Which do I choose for this poem? –
The yellow of a guinea, struck
to pay soldiers, or that of a
bowl an emperor took his rice from?
Neither. O give me the gold on the tongue
from a lemon picked when the day is young.

Blue

The blue door that the skylark opens –
a creaking of heavenly hinges.
The infinite recession of sky
painted blue by its own emptiness.
Metaphors for the ungraspable
essence of azure. 'Watch your pen,' is
what I say to myself. 'That colour
will run away with it, a mirage
of water in the yellow desert.
You will write of blue where there is none.'
Passing over the ocean, the
boat throws white spray from its bow. The wake
curves green behind. Looking down, you see
the brown of weed, the silver of fish
scattering from their pasture. The ink
flowing is blue-black, not blue as you think.

In Galleries

The guard has a right to despair. He stands by God
Being tickled by the Madonna; the baby laughs
And pushes himself away from his mother.
The lines and hollows of the piece of stone
Are human to people: their hearts go out to it.
But the guard has no one to make him human –
They walk through him as if he were a reflection.
The guard does not see them either, you are sure,
But he notices when someone touches something
And tells him not to; otherwise he stands
Blind, silent, among the people who go by
Indistinguishably, like minutes, like the hours.
Slowly the days go by, the years go by
Quickly: how many minutes does it take
To make a guard's hair uniformly grey?

But in Italy, sometimes, a guard is different.
He is poorer than a guard would be at home –
How cheap his old uniform is, how dirty!
He is a fountain of Italian:
He pulls back a curtain, shows you where to stand,
Cajoles you back to the Ludovisi Throne
To show you the side people forget to look at –
And exclaiming hopefully, vivaciously,
Bellissima! he shows you that in the smashed
Head of the crouching Venus the untouched lips
Are still parted hopefully, vivaciously,
In a girl's clear smile. He speaks and smiles;
And whether or not you understand Italian,
You understand he is human, and still hopes –
And, smiling, repeating his *Bellissima!*
You give him a dime's worth of aluminium.

You may even see a guard who is dumb, whose rapt
Smile, curtain-pulling-back, place indication,
Plain conviction that he guards a miracle
Are easier to understand than Italian.
His gestures are full of faith in – of faith.
When at last he takes a magnifying glass
From the shiny pocket of his uniform
And shows you that in the painting of a woman
Who holds in her arms the death of the world,
The something on the man's arm is the woman's
Tear, you and the man and the woman and the guard
Are dumbly one. You say *Bellissima!*
Bellissima! and give him his own rapt,
Dumb, human smile, convinced he guards
A miracle. Leaving, you hand the man
A quarter's worth of nickel and aluminium.

FLEUR ADCOCK

Leaving the Tate

Coming out with your clutch of postcards
in a Tate Gallery bag and another clutch
of images packed into your head you pause
on the steps to look across the river

and there's a new one: light bright buildings,
a streak of brown water, and such a sky
you wonder who painted it – Constable? No:
too brilliant. Crome? No: too ecstatic –

a madly pure Pre-Raphaelite sky,
perhaps, sheer blue apart from the white plumes
rushing up it (today, that is,
April. Another day would be different

but it wouldn't matter. All skies work.)
Cut to the lower right for a detail:
seagulls pecking on mud, below
two office blocks and a Georgian terrace.

Now swing to the left, and take in plane-trees
bobbled with seeds, and that brick building,
and a red bus . . . Cut it off just there,
by the lamp-post. Leave the scaffolding in.

That's your next one. Curious how
these outdoor pictures didn't exist
before you'd looked at the indoor pictures,
the ones on the walls. But here they are now,

marching out of their panorama
and queuing up for the viewfinder
your eye's become. You can isolate them
by holding your optic muscles still.

You can zoom in on figure studies
(that boy with the rucksack), or still lives,
abstracts, townscapes. No one made them.
The light painted them. You're in charge

of the hanging committee. Put what space
you like around the ones you fix on,
and gloat. Art multiplies itself.
Art's whatever you choose to frame.

DAVID HOLBROOK

Reflections on a Book of Reproductions

Hours are a small thing, the interior
(Woman at tub, lamps, Vermeer's whore,
Onions or spinets) insignificant

At the time, in Time. But magnificent
The art's consideration of the body,
Nymph bathing; model, now long decayed,
Become Christ off the cross; the maid
Spurning the lover's flowers; old man
Blowing his smoke rings, And if I can
I would lay out the patterns of mine
Into something more than these nine
Hours since I woke this morning, one
For lifting a tree-stump, one to run
A Ford van round the shops for meat,
For onions, for fruit, and the rest we ate;
Another for a child's rest; another
For the two little girls to go to shop with their mother.

Then we all gather round for the tea,
All laying claim to her, or informing me,
Under the candles, about how they bought
A pair of shoes, and how the bus they caught
Struck the branches of trees, and what
The old man in the seat behind
Said to his wife, while they sneezed and grinned.
Yet this is the family food of the aspiration
To celebrate order: Bach's elation
Was nourished on soup and hearth,
And worked among insolent men; the bath
That bathed the Badende Nymphe was crock;

Snyder's lobsters were stolen by cats; the clock
Muttered rustily in their rooms; their studio fires
Went out; cursed their wives, imperfectly fed their
    desires;
And the artist would swear at his daughters who sit so
    prim
In the Kaiser-Friedrich-Museum, for ever looking at him
With tender and timorous eyes beneath simple crowns of
    Flowers:
A Dutch interior is but as clean and simple as ours.

So we are not demeaned by simplicity, or banality,
By our cars, electric kettles, or lamps; the finality
Of our death, even, in the mass-produced chest:
Burial may ennoble us, that we watch our best
From time to time put in the ground. From such roots
We may draw from the soaring elms, the yellow
Pillars of poplar, as each great red ball sinks below
Our pathetic horizon, some share of the significance
The great painters saw, between the small hours and the
    natural world's magnificence.

GEOFFREY GRIGSON

Picture in a Closed Book

I keep a picture in a shut book,
A coloured lithograph, bound in.
Each time I open this shut book I think
Why don't I cut this splendid picture out
And hang it up inside a frame?
And at once I shut this book again.

Notes

EZRA POUND – *The Picture* – page 34
This painting of 'Venus reclining' or 'Venus with three putti' or 'An Allegory of Abundance' as it has been variously called, is considered by Pound scholars to be the picture to which Pound's poem refers. There are two versions of it, one in the National Gallery (London), the other in the Louvre. The painting is no longer attributed to Jacopo del Sellaio, it seems, but to an unnamed follower of Botticelli.

F.T. PRINCE – *Soldiers Bathing* – page 36
Michelangelo was commissioned in the autumn of 1504 to paint a battle scene for the Palazzo della Signoria in Florence as a companion piece to the 'Battle of Anghiari' ordered from Leonardo da Vinci several months earlier. The cartoon for the 'Battle of Cascina' was finished, at least in part, by early 1505 but Michelangelo was prevented from completing the work because he was urgently summoned to Rome by the Pope, Julius II, who wanted him to begin work on his tomb. All that remains of the project are some drawings and this copy of the cartoon. The work referred to in the third verse is probably an engraving, 'Battle of Nude Men', by Antonio Pollaiuolo.

WILLIAM CARLOS WILLIAMS – *The Dance* – page 44
This 'Peasant Dance', sometimes referred to as the 'Peasant Kermis', by Brueghel seems the likely source of inspiration for William Carlos Williams's poem. Williams studied in Vienna in 1924 when, presumably, he could have seen this painting. Another version of the 'Peasant Dance' with a more crowded composition is in the Detroit Institute of Arts and an early drawing, 'The Kermess of Hoboken', belongs to the Courtauld Institute.

PETER PORTER – *Looking at a Melozzo da Forì* – page 46
'The Annunciation' from the Pantheon in Rome which is the painting considered in the poem is no longer thought to be by Melozzo da Forì. Some scholars attribute it to Antoniazzo Romano, one of Melozzo's contemporaries.

THOM GUNN – *In Santa Maria del Popolo* – page 48
Caravaggio was not murdered as the poem appears to indicate but died of a fever at Porto Ercole in 1610.

B.C. LEALE – *Sketch by Constable* – page 82
According to the Catalogue of the Constable Exhibition at the Tate Gallery in 1976, 192, this oil sketch may have provided a source for the left-hand side of Constable's famous painting, 'The Hay-Wain', in the National Gallery.

ANTHONY CRONIN – *Lines for a Painter* – page 149
The name of the painter Patrick Swift may be unfamiliar to many readers. He was a friend to many poets some of whom he painted, among them John Heath Stubbs and David Gascoyne. He edited the magazine *X* with David Wright, and spent the last years of his life in Portugal, adamantly refusing to exhibit his paintings.

W.B. YEATS – *Leda and the Swan* – page 186
The identification of the source of Yeats's inspiration for this poem has been a fascinating investigation in which copies of Michelangelo's lost painting of 'Leda and the Swan' and Gustave Moreau's 'Leda' have figured among others. In the *Times Literary Supplement* of 20 July 1962, however, Charles Madge proposed that Yeats had in mind a relief formerly exhibited in the Etruscan Room at the British Museum as details in the poem corresponded closely to the details of the sculpture. (This is the object we have chosen to correspond with the poem.) Madge wrote that Yeats lived in Woburn Buildings, two minutes walk away from the British Museum, from 1895 to 1917. In the *Times Literary Supplement* of 3 August 1962, Giorgio Melchiori, a Yeats scholar who had written a great deal about the poet's visual sources, agreed with Madge's view and pointed out further evidence of the influence of the relief upon Yeats in earlier versions of the poem. On 9 November 1962, in the TLS, Charles B. Gullans pointed out a possible source for the poem in a woodcut by Yeats's friend, T. Sturge Moore (published in Modern Woodcutters No. 3, T. Sturge Moore 1921). He also pointed out that elements in an ode Sturge Moore wrote 'To Leda' are reflected in Yeats's poem. He proposed the very feasible suggestion that Yeats's imagination may have been stimulated by all three sources. We are indebted to Daniel Hoffman for drawing our attention to this information.

Acknowledgements

The publishers have made every effort to trace the ownership of copyright material in this book. It is their belief that the necessary permissions from publishers, author and authorised agents have been obtained, but in the event of any question arising as to the use of any material, the publishers, while expressing regret for any error unconsciously made, will be pleased to make the necessary correction in any future editions of this book.

Acknowledgments are due to the following for permission to reprint copyright material:

Anna Adams for 'Totes Meer – by Paul Nash 1940–41', © Anna Adams;

Fleur Adcock for 'Leaving the Tate' from WITH A POET'S EYE, published by the Tate Gallery, 1986;

Chatto & Windus for 'Uncertain Grace' from SPHERES by *James Aitchison*;

Carcanet Press Limited for 'Poor Boy: Portraits of a Painting' from THE GOODBYES by *John Ash*, Manchester 1982;

Faber and Faber Ltd and Random House, Inc for 'Musée des Beaux Arts' by *W. H. Auden* from COLLECTED POEMS and W.H. AUDEN: COLLECTED POEMS edited by Edward Mendelson, copyright 1940 and renewed 1968 by W.H. Auden;

McClelland and Stewart Limited, Toronto, for 'El Greco: Espolio' from SELECTED POEMS by *Earle Birney*;

Century Hutchinson Limited for 'Reflections on the Purchase by a Municipal Gallery of Three Heads by Henry Moore' from AN ATTITUDE OF MIND by *John Cassidy*;

Gillian Clarke for 'The Rothko Room' from WITH A POET'S EYE, published by the Tate Gallery, 1986;

Chatto & Windus for 'Old Movies' from OLD MOVIES AND OTHER POEMS by *John Cotton*;

Carcanet Press Limited for 'Lines for a Painter' from NEW & SELECTED POEMS by *Anthony Cronin*, © 1982 Anthony Cronin;

Martyn Crucefix for 'At the National Gallery';

Poetry Wales Press for 'Spring Fed' from LETTING GO by *Tony Curtis*;

Jonathan Cape Ltd and Wesleyan University Press for 'The Bird of Paradise' from THE COMPLETE POEMS of *W.H. Davies*, © Executors of the W.H. Davies Estate;

Anvil Press Poetry Ltd for 'Standing Female Nude' by *Carol Ann Duffy*;

Faber and Faber Ltd for 'War Blinded' from ST KILDA'S PARLIAMENT by *Douglas Dunn*;

Faber and Faber Ltd and Harcourt Brace Jovanovich, Inc. for 'Lines for Cuscuscaraway and Mirza Ali Beg' from COLLECTED POEMS 1909–1962 by *T.S. Eliot;*

D.J. Enright for 'God Creating Adam' from WITH A POET'S EYE published by the Tate Gallery, 1986;

Watson, Little for 'Home and Colonial' from COLLECTED POEMS by D.J. Enright, Oxford University Press;

Princeton University Press for 'Portrait of the Artist's Mother' from I, VINCENT: POEMS FROM THE PICTURES OF VAN GOGH by *Robert Fagles*, © 1978 by Robert Fagles;

Ruth Fainlight for 'Fire' from SIBYLS AND OTHERS, Hutchinson, 1980;

U.A. Fanthorpe for 'Not my Best Side' from SIDE EFFECTS, Henry Chambers/Peterloo Poets;

Vicki Feaver for 'Oi yoi yoi' from WITH A POET'S EYE published by the Tate Gallery, 1986;

Viking Penguin Inc. for the extract from 'Portrait de Femme' from NEW & SELECTED POEMS by *Irving Feldman*, © 1964 by Irving Feldman. Originally published in *The New Yorker;*

New Directions Publishing Corporation for 'Short Story on a Painting by Gustav Klimt' from ENDLESS LIFE by *Lawrence Ferlinghetti*, © 1976 by Lawrence Ferlinghetti;

John Fuller for 'The Money of their Colour';

Mrs Nessie Graham for 'The Thermal Stair' by W.S. Graham;

The Bodley Head for 'Helen' from HELEN OF EURIPEDES by *George Seferis* translated by Rex Warner;

Oxford University Press for 'Toulouse Lautrec at the Moulin Rouge' from OUT OF BOUNDS by *Jon Stallworthy*, © Oxford University Press 1963;

James MacGibbon for 'Spanish School' from THE COLLECTED POEMS of *Stevie Smith*, (Penguin Modern Classics);

Faber and Faber Ltd and Alfred A. Knopf, Inc. for the extract from 'The Man with the Blue Guitar' from THE COLLECTED POEMS of Wallace Stevens;

David Higham Associates Ltd for 'Do not go gentle into that good night' from COLLECTED POEMS by *Dylan Thomas*, published by J.M. Dent Ltd;

Macmillan, London and Basingstoke, for 'Threshold' from BETWEEN HERE AND NOW by *R.S. Thomas*;

Martin Secker & Warburg Ltd for 'The Bonfire' from POEMS 1958–1983 by *Anthony Thwaite*;

Oxford University Press for 'Paring the Apple' from COLLECTED POEMS by *Charles Tomlinson*, © Charles Tomlinson 1985;

John Wain for 'J.M.W. Turner: "The Shipwreck"';

Theodore Weiss for 'Ten Little Rembrandts', © Theodore Weiss;

Jon Manchip White for 'The Rout of San Romano';

Faber and Faber Ltd and Harcourt Brace Jovanovich, Inc. for 'Museum Piece' from POEMS 1943–1956 and CEREMONY AND OTHER POEMS by *Richard Wilbur*, © 1950, 1978 by Richard Wilbur;

New Directions Publishing Corporation for 'The Dance' from COLLECTED LATER POEMS by *William Carlos Williams*, © 1944;

A.D. Peters & Co. Ltd. for 'By the Effigy of St Cecilia' from TO THE GODS THE SHADES by *David Wright*, Carcanet Press;

A.P. Watt Ltd for 'The Municipal Gallery Revisited' and 'Leda and the Swan' from THE COLLECTED POEMS of *W.B. Yeats*, © Michael B. Yeats and Macmillan London Ltd.

Index of Poets

Index of Artists